The Land and People of
KOREA

KOREA, a small, mountainous land in northeastern Asia, has a long history that reflects the proximity of the great Asian powers. Korean art and culture had been influenced by China as early as the twelfth century B.C., and China helped bring about the unification of the separate Korean kingdoms in the seventh century A.D. In more recent times, China, Japan, and the Soviet Union have each played an important role in Korea's political development. After more than twelve hundred years of unity, the country was divided again in 1945, into the Republic of Korea in the south and the Democratic People's Republic in the north. In this new revision, the author describes the common heritage of the two countries that make up modern Korea, as well as the differences between them, and explores the prospects for the future.

PORTRAITS OF THE NATIONS SERIES

The Land and People of
KOREA

by S. E. Solberg

REVISED EDITION 1973

PORTRAITS OF THE NATIONS SERIES

J. B. LIPPINCOTT COMPANY
Philadelphia   New York

Thanks to Mrs. Bonnie R. Crown, Director of the Asian Literature Program of the Asia Society, for her sustained and sustaining interest in the life and culture of Korea.

For photographs on the following pages, the author gratefully credits: James B. Palais, 134, 138; Korean Consulate General, New York, 118, 124; Ministry of Public Information, Republic of Korea, 11, 15, 26, 28, 37, 65 66, 71, 77, 104, 105, 111, 127, 143, 144.

U.S. Library of Congress Cataloging in Publication Data

Solberg, S   E
    The land and people of Korea.

    (Portraits of the nations series)
    SUMMARY: An introduction to the history, government, traditions, and way of life of the people of Korea.
    1. Korea—Juvenile literature. [1. Korea] I. Title.
DS904.S6   1973   915.19'03'43   73-602
ISBN-0-397-31405-1

Map by Donald T. Pitcher

For Stacey

THAT SHE MAY REMEMBER

Contents

1

Korea: Land and People

Korea is a country that was already old when Columbus first sighted the Caribbean islands. By the time the United States had declared itself free from England, Korea had entered into a period of isolation from other nations that led our forefathers to dub her the "hermit nation." All that the West knew of Korea before the 1880s came from the reports of a few shipwrecked sailors and a group of French Catholic fathers who had worked their way into Korea as missionaries. In the 1880s Korea opened her ports to the world, but within thirty years Japan had annexed Korea. Up to the end of World War II the West knew Korea mainly as a Japanese colony. In 1945 Korea again appeared as a free nation in name, but divided by the course of the cold war into north and south, Russian and American zones. Today we know Korea best as a place where American soldiers fought from 1950 to 1953 and have been stationed ever since.

The Korean peninsula juts southward from the Asian mainland toward the southern Japanese island of Kyushu. It runs roughly six hundred miles north and south, between the thirty-fourth and forty-second parallels north latitude. From a wide base against the Asian continent the peninsula narrows down to a thin waist only 120 miles across, then broadens again to 160 miles. It separates the Sea of Japan on the east from the Yellow Sea on the west. The northern boundaries are formed mainly with Manchuria, with a short length meeting the Soviet Union to the east. To the south is the Korea Strait which separates Korea from the southern Japanese island.

The land border with Manchuria and the Soviet Union is marked by rivers flowing east and west from Paektu-san,* the Great White Mountain. The Tumen River flows to the east, the Yalu River to the west, and backing these rivers is a rugged mountain chain. The only easy routes into the peninsula from the Asian mainland lie along the narrow coastal plains at the mouths of the Yalu and Tumen.

The peninsula itself is one of the most mountainous areas in the world. It has been compared to a sea running high—range upon range of mountains like waves in a high wind. These peaks are a part of the great range of mountains that circle the Pacific, surging northward from the Andes in South America, through the Rockies, across eastern Siberia, and southward through Korea to the island chains of the South Pacific.

Mountains have played an important role in the history of Korea. The range that extends east and west across the northern border has served to isolate the peninsula from the continent.

---

*Korean names and words are sometimes romanized (spelled in our alphabet) in different ways; Paektu-san may sometimes be spelled Baegdu-san. Several sounds that occur in Korean have no English equivalents. Some authors indicate these by diacritical marks, and others spell them in a way they feel will make them easier to pronounce. The standard romanization, the McCune-Reischauer System, is used in his book, except for some place and personal names (Seoul, Park Chung Hee) which are given the spelling most commonly used.

Another range running north and south, and forming a kind of lopsided T with the east-west range, has helped to determine the pattern of settlement within the peninsula.

The north-south range of mountains holds close to the eastern side of the Korean peninsula, with lateral branches and spurs extending in a southwesterly direction. On either side of these rugged mountains lie the lowland areas. There is a narrow coastal plain along the eastern seaboard, with some lowlands following the course of the short rivers that run east to the sea. To the west of the mountains there is a much broader coastal plain with larger river basins, and in the southwest there are extensive plains.

The mountains have limited the amount of land that can be used for agriculture, and only 20 percent of the peninsula is arable. Since Korea is a country where over half the people depend on agriculture for a living, this means that the heaviest

Rice paddies.

population appears in the agricultural areas, the plains, and river basins.

In land area the Korean peninsula is about the same size as Minnesota, yet in that relatively small area live over 45 million people. Over 31 million of these people live in the southern parts of the peninsula in slightly less than a half of the total land area. In the agricultural areas, the southwest plain in particular, this means seven hundred people or more for every square mile of land.

Despite its small size the Korean peninsula shows a wide range of climate. Though all of Korea has what is called a midlatitude monsoonal climate, the topography and nearness or distance from the sea allow for a great diversity. While parts of the south are subtropical, the far north has a climate much like that of Siberia. In the summer, moist air drifts in from over the sea; in the winter, dry cold air drifts outward from the continent of Asia.

Around Seoul, the capital of the Republic of Korea, which lies about halfway down the western side of the peninsula, the climate is moderate. The hottest summer months have an average temperature of seventy-seven degrees Fahrenheit and the coldest winter months twenty-three degrees. In the central far north there are areas where summer temperatures average under seventy degrees, and the winter averages are around zero. On the southern tip the winter averages are around freezing, and there are some areas where many winters will pass without a severe frost.

Korean rains are monsoonal; over half of Korea's rainfall comes during three months in summer—June, July, and August. Sometimes as much as 30 percent of the annual rainfall comes in July alone. For most of the country this means fifteen to twenty inches of rain in three months, more than the annual rainfall in many parts of the United States. But despite heavy rains Korean

Spring Landscape,
a late Yi dynasty painting
by Yi In-mun.

summer averages seven to eight hours of sunshine a day. This means it rains very hard during the remaining hours.

Seasons in Korea are clearly marked. Spring comes with the pink of flowering azaleas on the hillsides and the yellow flashes of forsythia. The raw winds of March turn warm, and the hills and fields begin to green. Summer follows quickly, temperatures rise, and by late June or early July the rains have begun. There is little cooling with the rains, and rain or not, a hot day is hot.

By late summer the rice paddies are beginning to ripen and yellow, the heat has settled down, and the constant shrill humming of the cicadas in the trees makes it even harder than usual to stay awake on hot lazy afternoons. The rains are over, and the harvest time is approaching. The only dark spots in the sky are the clouds that mark the approach of typhoons from the Pacific. They come most often in August, and usually they miss Korea.

But when they do hit they bring winds and heavy rains that wreck villages and crops and cause disastrous floods.

Fall months are the best time of the year. The skies are clear and blue; "high sky" is the Korean phrase. Evenings are cool and the days not so hot. It is time for picnics and trips to view the autumn colors in the mountains, a time when nature is at her best, particularly if there has been a good harvest.

In most of Korea the real cold comes late, around January. The winter snows pile high in the north; in the south there is little snow. Yet the cold winds that drive down from the central Asian plains chill the air; even as spring approaches and the temperatures rise, the dry cold winds turn raw and blustery. Then suddenly the pink of azalea appears and it is spring again.

In this basically agricultural country, there are still relatively few cities. Those which have grown up on the Korean peninsula represent administrative and commercial centers such as Seoul, the capital of the Republic of Korea, and P'yŏngyang, the capital of the Democratic People's Republic of Korea; ports, such as Pusan at the southern tip, Inch'ŏn, the port for Seoul, or Wŏnsan on the northeast coast; and inland distribution centers such as Taegu in the south central plains.

Korea's natural resources are relatively limited in variety and amount, and, in many cases, poorly developed. For an agricultural country her soil is poor; the mountains are relatively young and rich topsoils have not had time to develop. Korean soils have had to be made by the farmers, built up by centuries of cultivation and fertilization. This means that large amounts of fertilizers, both chemical and organic, are required to maintain food production.

Mineral resources are limited, but Korea does have rather good deposits of iron, coal, gold, silver, and tungsten. It is important to note that the essentials for developing heavy industry, coal and iron, are almost all found in the north. The south does have some coal which is used for fuel and to fire steam plants to generate electricity. Gold and tungsten are the major minerals mined in the south today.

Short rivers running quickly down to the sea from the rough mountains have a great potential for development as hydro-electric power. More has been done to harness this potential in the north than in the south.

Today the mountains, which once were covered with rich forests, are nearly bare over much of the country. It is only in the northeast that major stands of timber still remain.

The seas around the Korean peninsula are rich in seafood. In particular the Japan Sea, where there is a meeting of cold and warm currents, produces a great variety of fish. Fishing villages dot the east coast where the coastal plain is too narrow to permit any extensive agriculture. The major catch includes sardine, mackerel, anchovy, and herring. Together with these are shrimp, clams and oysters, abalone, and several kinds of edible seaweeds.

Tungsten mine in the Republic of Korea.

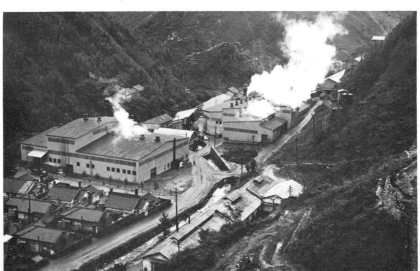

Most fishing is carried on in small boats, although both North and South Korea are developing modern fishing fleets. Around the island of Cheju-do, off the southwest tip of the peninsula, women are famous as divers, scouring the bottom of the sea for pearl oysters, shellfish, and other sea foods.

The people who live on the Korean peninsula are of mixed origin. They arrived from the north in prehistoric times, most probably as a part of the great migrations that swept across Manchuria and Siberia and on into North America. Later there were migrations from the Central Asian plains and China.

Geographical position has played a major role in the history of Korea. As a peninsula, cut off from the continent by rough mountains and seas, she has often been able to isolate herself from what was happening on the mainland. On the other hand, Korea is located in a position of prime importance for military control of Manchuria or China. She has been a small country caught between major powers, "a shrimp caught between two fighting whales," as the Koreans say.

Mongolian armies have descended upon her on their way to attack Japan. Japan has sent armies across Korea to attack China, both in the sixteenth and nineteenth centuries. Then, as the power of czarist Russia grew in Asia, Japan again sent her troops into Korea, and having sent them kept them on, finally to annex Korea as a colony. Today this peninsula is divided along an uncertain armistice line after enduring the troops of many nations fighting on her soil in a hot battle in the cold war.

But the peninsula also served as a route for things more valuable than armies. Korea was closer to the great culture centers of eastern and central Asia than Japan. And in the course of the centuries much that was valuable from those civilizations—ideas, skills, and religions—came down the Korean land bridge, there to be modified to fit Korean needs, and sent on to Japan.

2

The Beginnings

All the world's great civilizations have grown from four centers. The oldest was the center that grew up on the banks of the Tigris, the Euphrates, and the Nile, and from which we trace the direct descent of the tradition which today we call Western. The second great center of civilization grew up on the banks of a source of the Yellow River in China. From it sprang the East Asian tradition, which today includes China, Japan, Korea, and much of Southeast Asia. The third civilization center was along the banks of the Indus River. From it came the great civilization of India which influenced all of Southeast Asia and much of East Asia. The fourth was the Mayan civilization in Central America. Its tradition was very nearly brought to an end by the arrival of the Spanish conquerors.

When we look at our own history it is clear that for many thousands of years Western civilization had little contact with that of East Asia or with the Mayan. It was not until the thirteenth century, with the Mongols attacks on Europe, that a real awareness of the power and richness of Asian civilization began to develop in the West. Within two centuries merchants and missionaries began to push their way east, and soon, of course, west, in search for a short cut to the East.

China resisted the advances of the West. She closed her ports to foreign ships, and it was not until 1842 that China was forced open by the West. Japan and Korea followed the same course. In 1854 Japan began to open her ports, and it was not until 1882 that Korea followed.

As the last of these nations to open her door to the West, Korea remained the one least influenced by the West. When we turn to Korea's history we are looking at a civilization that for most of recorded history has had very little to do with our world. The life of the Korean we look at today belongs to another tradition, one that only recently has begun to borrow from the Western tradition with which we are familiar.

There is little information about the first men on the Korean peninsula. There were men in the Chinese Yellow River basin at least five hundred thousand years ago. Successive migrations from there crossed over to the North American mainland by way of Manchuria and Siberia, and some no doubt came south into the Korean peninsula, perhaps even crossing over to Japan. The original population of the Korean peninsula was most probably built up by waves of small migrations from north central Asia which spread over a very long period, perhaps as much as fifty thousand years.

A Korean legend puts the founding of the Korean nation at a very specific date, 2400 B.C. At that time a son of the Creator is supposed to have promised to grant human form to a tiger and a bear if they would meet certain demands, among them spending one hundred days in a dark cave. The tiger was unable to last out the hundred days, but the bear did and was metamorphosed into a woman. The Creator's son was attracted to this woman, and she bore him a son, Tangun. Tangun is said to have brought together the tribes around Paektu-san, the Great White Mountain which now marks the northern boundary of Korea, and to have given them laws, and ruled over them.

Modern historians feel that there is a grain of truth in this legend. It would appear that sometime around 2000 B.C. a leader appeared who was able to bring several scattered groups together to form the beginnings of a state.

The next date that becomes important in the records of Korea's early history is the fall of the Shang dynasty in China. Around 1200 B.C. Kija, a minister of that dynasty, is said to have come to Korea with a large following. He is supposed to have founded a kingdom in the Taedong River basin, near present day P'yŏngyang. Whether he did or not, the important fact remains that at this time there was a great influx of Chinese technology and customs into the northern part of the peninsula and bordering Manchurian areas.

Over the following centuries there was a steady flow of influence from the more highly developed Chinese civilization into the northwestern parts of what is today Korea and the areas to the north and west that were a part of Korea at that time. Rice, barley, and wheat were introduced, laws were established, and the system of land division used in the collecting of taxes was the same as that used in China. Land was cut up into sections containing nine equal squares, one in the middle surrounded by the eight others. The produce of the center square went to the government as a kind of tax. Writing is said to have been introduced from China during this time, but no Korean written records remain.

The tribes and small states that were to be brought together to make up Korea were scattered up and down the peninsula. They had all advanced beyond primitive agriculture. Each had its own social and political organization and lived in a fairly well defined area. They had developed religions, had horses, cattle, pigs, and raised some grains. The more advanced among them cultivated hemp, flax, and mulberry for silkworms, though some of the groups did not make cloth and instead dressed in skins. But to the Chinese, upon whose records we have to depend for the description of these ancestors of the modern Koreans, they were all barbarians who were extremely fond of singing, dancing, and drinking.

Nonwritten records, to which the archeologist turns in his search for the past, confirm pretty well what we know from the Chinese histories. Stone Age remains have been found scattered all along the peninsula, confirming the early presence of man there. Two types of pottery that have been found are of interest. One is the same as that found throughout Manchuria and Mongolia, serving to confirm speculation that the early people on the peninsula came from that area. The other shows a strong similarity to pottery found in northern China and helps to acknowledge the early presence of Chinese influence within the peninsula.

Sometime between the second and third millenniums B.C., the period of the legendary Tangun, some copper artifacts such as swords begin to appear along with stone implements. This was the time when the step from the stone age to that of metals was beginning, perhaps as the result of the immigration of some more highly developed people who brought their skills with them.

Early in the second century B.C. many Chinese intellectuals fled China following an order by the emperor that all Confucian books be burned. Along with them came many of the common people who were being forced by the same emperor to build the Great Wall of China.

It was during this period that the kingdom said to be founded by Kija collapsed. It appears to have been a small city-state that fell before the attack of a leader named Wiman who was able to bring a much larger area under his control. Strong leaders were emerging who could combine more and more of the independent groups that lived on the Korean peninsula and in the bordering Manchurian areas.

But these were no great and glittering kingdoms. We must always remember that the further back from our time we go, the slower the pace of change. Ten years or less in our world probably includes more change than five hundred years did in the world we have been discussing. Wiman's Korea was still a mixed stone and metal culture. It was not until his kingdom fell to the Han dynasty Chinese in 108 B.C. that Korea emerged fully into the metal age.

The Chinese divided the northern areas of the peninsula into four prefectures, the most important of which was known as Nangnang. They did not maintain control over the area for long, however. Within twenty-five years two of the original four prefectures were no longer under effective Chinese control, and by 37 B.C. China had relinquished control on the peninsula, although Nangnang continued to exist for another three hundred years.

3

Three Kingdoms Made into One

By the beginning of the Christian era three independent kingdoms had begun to take form on the peninsula. To the north was Koguryŏ, 37 B.C. to A.D. 668, its boundaries extending north into present-day Manchuria and south to the narrow waist of the peninsula. To the southwest was Paekche, 18 B.C. to A.D. 660, taking up the southwest quarter of the peninsula. To the southeast was Silla, 57 B.C. to A.D. 935, taking up more or less the rest of the peninsula. These are the commonly accepted dates for these kingdoms and serve only to give a general idea of the time they existed.

In their early centuries these three kingdoms were kept busy trying to gain control of the many different peoples living on the peninsula and establishing firm boundaries. Later, when their boundaries began to touch, they were to engage in bloody border wars until the Silla kingdom unified the peninsula in the seventh century.

To the north, Koguryŏ grew up next to the Han dynasty Chinese colonies and continued to develop alongside Nangnang for the next three hundred years. Then, even after absorbing Nangnang, Koguryŏ was faced with China to the west. From the north there was the constant danger of attack by the warlike

Astronomical observatory, among the oldest in the world, built in seventh-century Silla.

Manchurian peoples. Existence was dependent upon strong defense, and soon Koguryŏ grew into an aggressive, warring state. In the height of her glory she was able to repulse invasion attempts by the full strength of China and even to harbor dreams of aggression against her powerful western neighbor.

Located in an area which had been largely under Chinese control and constantly in touch with the Chinese culture center to the west, Koguryŏ adapted much that was Chinese to her way of life. For while she might well have resented Chinese military advances, she did not fail to acknowledge Chinese cultural superiority. Still, respect for a cultural superior does not always mean slavish imitation—and though the few remains we have of Koguryŏ today do show the marked influence of the Chinese Han dynasty, they are also indicative of a strongly creative people who were able to take what they learned and build upon it.

Perhaps the most striking remains of the northern kingdom—and a testimony of the Chinese colonies that preceded it—have been found in the excavation of tombs. Tombs have been discovered near P'yŏngyang, the ancient capital of Koguryŏ, along the Manchurian border, and elsewhere in northern Korea. They consist of stone-walled chambers where the bodies were placed. The chamber itself was then piled over with earth to make a large mound. From the outside these tombs are not very imposing, but once the stone door is passed, a universe in miniature is revealed. Each tomb was in fact conceived as a universe. The chambers were decorated with pictures of the sun, moon, and constellations, together with a representation of a celestial being, or god. Around the walls were scenes from the dead man's life: hunting, feasting, battle, his wife, his achievements, and his pleasures.

Unfortunately for us, the paintings are about all that have remained. The stone construction of the tombs made them easy of access, and they fell prey to grave-robbers over the centuries who denuded them of the wealth of jewelry, ornaments, and other artifacts they may have contained.

But the paintings themselves are a rich heritage. They reveal a great deal of skill in design and use of color. These are details of plants and foliage worked into intricate designs, stylized animals, and an overall sense of design and balance that are equal to any other fourth- or fifth-century Asian art that has come down to us.

Besides giving graphic representation of life in Koguryŏ and the Han colony of Nangnang, these paintings point to the cosmopolitan nature of the civilization that was developing on the peninsula. Though the major influence upon Korea was, and would remain, China, elements of other cultures were already entering in. It was out of this cultural richness, originating in China, central Asia, or Manchuria, that Korea was to pass on important elements to Japan. And in some cases, such as dance and music, the influence of this combined peninsular culture was to be felt even in China.

In one of the Koguryŏ tomb paintings there appears a dancer performing a dance that is of central Asian, or perhaps even Indian, origin. The dancer appears to be wearing a turban and is not Korean or Chinese. This tomb was constructed nearly fifty years before the date usually given for the introduction of Buddhism into Koguryŏ, and thus would seem to indicate that central Asian cultural patterns had begun to influence Korea even before the major influence of Buddhism.

Buddhism was introduced into Koguryŏ from China in 327, later to the other two kingdoms on the peninsula, and by way of Paekche, to Japan. It was to become one of the most important organized religions in Korea as well as the fountainhead of much of her truly great art. In popular forms it appealed to the common people through promises of salvation; for the intellectuals it provided a highly complex and difficult theology. It seems to have entered Korea first in its more sophisticated forms and only later to have become a popular religion.

The second kingdom of this period, Paekche, was located in the southwest of the peninsula which protected her from the warlike tribes to the north of Koguryŏ, and she did not find it necessary to develop along military lines. Though Koguryŏ cut her off from direct land contact with northern China, Paekche maintained close and generally friendly ties with southern China and Japan by sea.

In July, 1971, excavation of the tomb of King Muryong, twenty-fifth king of Paekche (reigned A.D. 501-523), revealed much new material for the understanding of Paekche culture.

The tomb, arched like a railway tunnel, is about three and three-quarters yards long; it is built of brick and roofed with tile. Here is clear evidence that by the sixth century Paekche artisans had achieved good control of many materials. Sophisticated techniques in the use of stone, bricks, tile, wood, plaster, and bronze are in evidence.

The tomb was fronted by a guardian stone lion; to the right were the remains of the king's coffin of lacquered wood; to the left that of the queen. There were many gold ornaments, pieces of jewelry, a bronze mirror, and bronze censer. Two gold crowns of very fine workmanship were also found. They are in the shape

Eighth-century pagoda at Puyo, capital of Paekche.

of flowers and flames. The high level of Paekche's artistic achievement, only hinted at by the few objects of sculpture known
before, has been fully confirmed by these findings.

Paekche is also said to have excelled in architecture, though
before this excavation there were hardly an architectural remains known on the Korean peninsula. Examples of this skill
survive, ironically enough, in Japan. The Horyuji temple at Nara
was built by Paekche artisans, and the imposing Kudara Kwanon,
a graceful wood sculpture larger than life, was worked from a
single block of wood by Paekche artists living in Japan.

Protected by mountains and the sea, the kingdom of Silla was
able to remain relatively undisturbed in its early years. Silla had
little direct contact with China overland, for Koguryŏ stood in
the way, and little contact by sea, for the west coast ports that
traded with China were in Paekche's territory. But at the same
time the area where this kingdom developed was the settling
ground for one of the most extensive early Chinese migrations
into the peninsula.

In the early centuries of Silla's growth this kingdom was seldom an aggressor, being rather content to protect itself from
outside attack. Yet it was Silla that was finally to rise and bring
most of what is modern Korea under one government.

Many modern Koreans would say that the real Korea began
with Silla. For as people find it necessary to look to the past for
ideals on which to base present action, so many Koreans have
taken Silla to their hearts as epitomizing bravery, courage, loyalty, and high intellectual accomplishment.

By the fifth century Silla had grown powerful enough to pose a
threat to Koguryŏ and Paekche, and serious trouble began to
break out along the frontiers. Whereas Paekche and Koguryŏ had
been constantly at loggerheads, Silla had managed to stay out of
most of the battles, although Silla had occasionally come to

When Silla and T'ang invaded Paekche, according to legend, ladies threw themselves into the Paengma River from this bluff, The Rock of Falling Flowers, to avoid capture.

Paekche's aid against the stronger northern state. It was Silla's skill in diplomacy, and particularly the ability to maintain strong ties based on mutual interest with China, that allowed her to dominate the power struggle on the peninsula.

In the second decade of the seventh century the Chinese Sui dynasty launched an attack on Koguryŏ. It resulted in an overwhelming defeat for the Chinese and hastened the downfall of Sui. Silla was cautious in establishing ties with the new T'ang dynasty that replaced Sui in 618, but by the time Paekche launched an attack on Silla in 642, Silla was able to call upon T'ang to aid in her defense.

The combined forces of T'ang and Silla quickly overthrew the Paekche kingdom and then moved against the more powerful northern kingdom of Koguryŏ. Koguryŏ fell in 668, leaving Silla and T'ang in control of the whole peninsula. China, with the memory of her colonial control in Han times, would of course have liked to remain. But she soon found it was impossible to maintain control of the territory. She did try, however, and at times open war broke out between Silla and T'ang. Silla demonstrated her growing power by turning back a Chinese invasion force. By the ninth century Silla was in firm control of most of the territory which is Korea today.

Silla became well known in the East. Scholars and Buddhist priests went to China to study. Commerce flourished: as early as the middle of the ninth century Arab geographers were aware of Silla, which they called "al-Sh-ila." Writing in 846, one of them noted, "At the furthest limit of China near Quansu are many mountains and many kings, and this is the land of al-Sh-ila in which there is much gold. He who enters it of the Moslems settles in it because of its excellence."

A rich and complex culture was developing on the peninsula. Buddhism spurred on the arts, scholars went to China to study, and the ethical system of Confucius and the scholarship that went along with Confucian studies were developed. A group of young men who gathered together to study, play, and learn the arts of war were known as the *hwarang*. The military spirit of the hwarang, their sense of loyalty to king and nation, and their refusal to accept defeat on the battlefield have led to the suggestion that the hwarang indeed were the unifiers of Silla.

Kim Yu-sin, the great general of the wars of unification, was trained as a hwarang. When one of his sons retreated from a battle General Kim disowned him, for no hwarang worth the name would leave the battlefield alive after losing the battle. Even though the king of Silla readily forgave the young man, General Kim never would, nor would the young man's mother, who argued, after her husband Kim Yu-sin died, that though a woman must obey three masters—father, husband, and son—since her husband had disowned their son, she could never accept the unfortunate young man as her son, either. The warrior code was indeed a strict and bitter one.

Pulguk-sa, Buddhist temple dating from Silla.

However, there was another and more pleasant side to the life of the hwarang. They often went in groups to the mountains, both for physical training and to enjoy the beauties of nature. They were highly literate, often wrote poetry, and engaged in artistic, intellectual, and political affairs as well as war. They were a stabilizing force in the society, producing a group of men trained in the same way and pledged to the same ideals and goals, from which Silla could draw her leaders in time of peace and generals in time of war.

The hwarang may well have had their origins in the original spirit worship of the peninsula. Later on elements of Confucianism and Buddhism entered into their makeup also. For Silla was no slavish imitator of outside cultures. She mixed them together with local customs and beliefs, creating something that was more Korean. This is, of course, another reason why modern Koreans look back to Silla: while they may admire Koguryŏ for her strength and Paekche for her refinement, Silla alone seems to have been truly Korean.

Yet even with her highly developed intellectual life and the great skill she demonstrated in some of the arts, Silla remained a land of villages where the farmer went out every day to his fields and came home every night if all went well. Agriculture was the economic base of the kingdom as it has been in Korea down into our century.

By 918 the court of Silla was dead, sapped by the internal corruption and wasteful living of its rulers. By 935 even her name had disappeared, for Silla had surrendered to the strongest of the many rebels who had led forces which ate away at her territory during the declining years.

These events were in part precipitated by the action of a Buddhist monk, Kung-ye, said to have been a son of one of Silla's kings. He had gained power as a leader of rebel (some would say bandit) forces, and as he was able to gain control over more territory he began more and more to feel the pleasures of power. First he took the title of "Great General" for himself, then in 901 designated himself king of all the territory under his control.

Along with the rise of his political and military power, Kung-ye became more and more involved in his Buddhist pursuits, eventually even to the point of calling himself an incarnation of the Buddha. Anyone who dared voice doubts about him or his policies was put to death, including his wife and sons.

Kung-ye was both feared and hated, and as he grew nearer to what seemed madness, more and more of the actual leadership of his armies fell upon the shoulders of a brilliant young leader, Wang Kŏn, who was respected as both general and civil governor in the territories where he had served. Wang Kŏn was urged to help overthrow Kung-ye, but refused to have anything to do with the plot. It was only by force that he was placed upon the throne which was wrested from Kung-ye. Wang Kŏn established his court in Songdo, better known today as Kaesŏng, and named his kingdom Koryŏ. In 920, Silla recognized Koryŏ as an independent kingdom and sent an envoy with gifts.

In the following years the Silla court continued to weaken. In the end the king of Silla saw no way to maintain his kingdom any longer. He decided to abdicate and handed over what was left of Silla to Wang Kŏn in 935.

Wang Kŏn accepted the abdication with courtesy and treated the former king of Silla with every dignity, gave him one of his daughters as wife, and appointed him to a sinecure in the Koryŏ government. Thus the kingdom which had unified the Korean peninsula and had produced some of its finest accomplishments in the arts came to an end. A new dynasty had taken power, that of Wang, and a new kingdom ruled the land, Koryŏ.

4

Koryŏ

The kingdom of Koryŏ, from which we derive our name for the peninsula, Korea, lasted from 918 to 1392. It was to see the flourishing of Buddhism, a great increase of skill in foreign relations, and the development of a bureaucratic state, together with the subjugation of Korea by the Mongols. Under the influence of Buddhism the arts flourished, including that of the potter who produced wares for use in the temples. Under the influence of Confucianism and Chinese thought, scholarship flourished and the political system became more sophisticated.

In general the kings of Koryŏ attempted to maintain close diplomatic connections with China. This was to their advantage when the Chinese were relatively strong and able to maintain control of the troublesome peoples to the north. When Chinese power weakened, Koryŏ's position did, too. Unfortunately for the Koryŏ kings they were ruling during a period when the Chinese power was at a low level and the groups in Manchuria and Mongolia were relatively strong.

It was only natural that in the course of their juggling for power in their own areas, the groups in Manchuria and Mongolia should look toward Korea, and a good part of the history of the Koryŏ kingdom is the story of attack and counterattack, and of the development of the diplomatic skills necessary for existence on the edge of a troubled area.

The first group to cause major trouble was known as the Kitan. War broke out with Koryŏ in 993. Although Koryŏ did not suffer military defeat, the king was forced to accept the overlordship of the Kitan ruler. Early in the eleventh century war broke out again. Fighting continued until 1020 when a period of stable diplomatic relations between the Kitan and Koryŏ began.

In the relatively quiet one hundred and fifty years that followed, sometimes called her golden age, Koryŏ was able to get back on her feet. The Koryŏ court had been unable to centralize power, and widely scattered centers of learning and local control grew up around the headquarters of strongmen. In the twelfth century this development led to the spreading of Chinese learning from the court all over the land. Local schools that had been in existence from the end of the tenth century now became larger and better.

Early in the twelfth century a powerful new kingdom, the Chin, came to power in Manchuria and Northern China. Korea accepted a subservient position, and this helped guarantee peace along the northern frontier.

But despite this bow to the power of Chin, Koryŏ continued to maintain her relationships with the Sung dynasty in the south of China. Koryŏ's ports were visited by ships, not only from Sung China and Japan, but even those of Arabian countries to the far west. The aristocrats of Koryŏ found Sung and Arabian fineries as much to their taste as the scholars found Sung books. In exchange major Koryŏ exports were gold, silver, and ginseng.

Koryŏ's first king, Wang Kŏn, had claimed that his kingdom had been founded by the help of the Buddha. Buddhism was protected by the court, temples flourished, and monks were influential in government affairs. The aristocratic class that grew up around the new court, and who held the most important government positions, grew wealthy. These aristocrats were patrons of the Buddhist temples and of the arts. It was during this 150-year golden age that the great production of Koryŏ ceramics took place.

With state support, Buddhist temples had important land holdings. Monks were not taxed; they engaged in money-lending and the making of wines for sale. Buddhism thus became an economic as well as spiritual influence in Koryŏ. On the political side, monks were influential in the court; kings deferred to them, and members of the royal family became monks themselves.

But, though Buddhism as a religion remained a force in Koryŏ, it did not supply the need for the practical day-to-day administration of government. It was the knowledge of Confucian ethics and the practical grounds for administration growing out of them that led to office and position.

In 957 Koryŏ had established a state examination system, on the model of the one in China, which was to be passed by all applicants for government service. Although the subjects of the examinations varied over the centuries, the basic questions were those centered on Confucian studies.

Government service was the final aim of the scholar. It was the way to position, prestige, and wealth, and a scholar's position made it impossible for him to go into business or any of the professions. To be a scholar was to serve the king and the government.

There were two branches of government service, the civil and the military. The civil was considered more important and was granted more prestige. Feeling grew among the military that they were being discriminated against, and finally in 1170 they led a revolt which put the civilian aristocrats out of power.

This revolt was to have far-reaching effects. Up to this time, only aristocrats had been able to receive government appointments, but now these became open to nearly anyone who could pass the examinations. Yet the reverberations of the overthrow of aristocratic power were even greater. All over the peninsula riots and revolts broke out. These were difficult years for Koryŏ, and a bitter foretaste of the future.

The thirteenth century saw the rise of the Mongol power that was to strike fear into all the civilized world. Begun by Genghis Khan, the empire spread within half a century over nearly all the Asian continent and well into Europe. It was with this growing power that Koryŏ had to contend.

In the beginning Koryŏ's relations with the Mongols were good. When Genghis Khan fought the Kitan, Koryŏ had given him aid. But the Koryŏ court was not farsighted enough to follow up this advantage. They treated Mongol envoys with contempt, and in 1231 the Mongols attacked. Koryŏ was badly defeated and signed a peace treaty in order to gain time to prepare for further defense.

The government moved to the island of Kanghwa, just across from the mouth of the Han River on the west coast of the peninsula. Quite naturally the Mongols became suspicious of the Koryŏ court's intentions. They returned to the attack in force.

No matter how well equipped their armies might have been for fighting on land, the Mongols did not have any ships, and they were never able to take the island fortress. But, though the Koryŏ government never fell to the Mongols, the Mongol armies did as they wished on the mainland, demolishing and pillaging. By 1238 the people of the peninsula were in a desperate condition, and many, following the pattern of their king, fled to the islands off the coasts.

The court remained on Kanghwa Island, the people suffered, and the overall situation changed very little despite the urgings of certain moderates in the court to come to terms with the Mongols. Instead the court launched a project it hoped would unite the Korean people against the Mongols, by giving them a spiritual basis for unity in Buddhism.

The Buddha was the protector of the kingdom. Early in the Koryŏ period, in 1011, a collection of Buddhist scriptures had been carved on woodblocks to be printed as a gesture of thanks to the Buddha for saving the country from invasion. Now the invading Mongols had destroyed the original woodblocks, and the

Eighty thousand hand-carved wooden printing blocks of Buddhist scriptures, preserved since the eleventh century.

court ordered a new compilation of the scriptures to be made and a new set of blocks to be carved.

The work consumed seventeen years and the efforts of hundreds of scholars and technicians, but finally enough woodblocks were carved to print 160,000 pages. These woodblocks are still preserved in a Buddhist temple, the Haein-sa, in southern Korea.

By the time the woodblocks were carved, however, the court had capitulated to the Mongols and had returned to its capital on the mainland. In 1259 began the suzerainty of Korea to the Mongols that continued down into the fourteenth century. During these years the court was but a show. Kings were forced to marry Mongol princesses, and the government was modified along Mongol lines. Officials of the Mongol government were stationed in Korea to supervise the activities of the Korean government.

In 1273 and again in 1282 the Mongols launched unsuccessful attacks on Japan. In preparation for these attacks they recruited Korean troops and manpower and forced the building of ships on the Korean peninsula. This created an additional burden on a country that was already suffering from the effects of extended war and internal revolts, as well as the raids of Japanese pirates which had begun on a large scale in the second decade of the thirteenth century.

The Mongol domination was not all bad, however. Through contacts with the Mongol capital at Karakorum the culture of the world was made available to the Korean scholars. Here was the center of a vast empire that brought together the varied cultures of all the civilized world. Scholars from Korea were brought into contact with the medicine, astronomy, mathematics, and other sciences and arts of the West. And Korean culture itself had its influence in return, for the skill of Koryŏ's artists and craftsmen was first brought to the world's attention at Karakorum.

The Mongol domination also led to a centralization of authority in the capital. The power of the scattered strongmen was being broken, and along with it went the growing internal trade and developing money economy. At the same time profound social changes were taking place. The relatively democratic military hierarchy had allowed for a good deal of social movement; the same was true of the Buddhist hierarchy. Commoners were able to hold important positions.

As the Mongols' power began to wane the Chinese shook free, and the Ming dynasty was established in 1368. This brought immediate changes in Korea. An anti-Mongol group in the court used the occasion to have the king disclaim the overlordship of the Mongols and establish relations with Ming. But the pro-Mongol forces were soon in control again. In 1388 the Koryŏ king dispatched an army against Ming China.

The king could not have picked a worse time to launch this attack. For years the country had been drained by the attacks of Japanese pirates—raids that at times looked more like invasions as the raiders gained confidence and even threatened the capital at Kaesŏng. There had been constant small wars with Manchurian groups along the northern frontiers. The king and court had done little to relieve the suffering of the people. While farmers were starving, the king would ride across their lands, trampling down the crops, on hunting trips with his retinue. The court was sunk in pleasure-seeking debauchery.

During these years of hardship a strong leader was coming up, General Yi Sŏng-gye. He helped put down the northern tribes and was very successful against the Japanese raiders. A skilled general, he is pictured as a furious warrior, a skilled marksman with the bow, who was always in the front of battle mounted on his white horse. He fast became a national hero, a man the people knew and respected. He was also a firm supporter of the pro-Ming faction around the court.

When the king ordered the generals to march against Ming, General Yi Sŏng-gye argued against the action. He protested that it was foolish for a small country to attack a large one; that the summer was a poor time to begin an attack, for the long heavy rains made roads impassable and the heat and damp would ruin the bows; and moreover, that it was foolish to pull troops out of Korea when the Japanese were continually raiding.

The king's only reply was that the next man who objected to his decision would be beheaded. The troops were ordered to march north. General Yi was seen to weep, for, he said, this meant the end of Koryŏ.

General Yi led his troops to an island near the mouth of the Yalu and went into camp there. He did not move any further against China, and finally, after trying once more to get the king to change his mind, General Yi Sŏng-gye put the question to his troops: Should they move against Ming China or march back on the capital? The troops were wholeheartedly in support of the move against the Korean capital.

The decision was made, but even as General Yi sat on his white horse watching his troops cross back to the Koryŏ side of the river he seems to have had no thought of overthrowing the dynasty; rather, he hoped to save it from what he considered a fatal mistake.

Events were to take a different course, however. Within four years the general who had served the Koryŏ kingdom so well for so long was placed on the throne through the efforts of his son. The reforms he had begun during those four years as the most powerful man in the kingdom were to be carried forward by a new dynasty, founded in July of 1392. Yi Sŏng-gye was its first king.

5

Chosŏn: The Yi Dynasty

The Yi dynasty which Yi Sŏng-gye founded, one hundred years before Columbus first sighted America, lasted until 1910 when Korea became a colony of Japan. This period saw a major development in the intellectual life of the peninsula linked with the state support of Confucianism; developments in the arts and literature; two devastating invasions, one by the Japanese, the other by the Manchus; and the opening of Korea by Japan and to the West.

One of Yi Sŏng-gye's first moves after he took the throne was to ask approval of his reign from the Ming emperor. The emperor granted investiture to the new king and also approved the name Chosŏn for the new kingdom. Thus, unified Korea had existed under three different names: Silla, Koryŏ, and Chosŏn. Relationships with Ming China continued to be generally good, with none of the political subservience that had characterized the Mongol domination of Korea.

Once he was firmly on the throne the new king set about establishing land reforms, strengthening the administrative structure, stabilizing the northern border against the ever troublesome Manchurian groups, and developing his new capital city, present-day Seoul.

In general, the first two hundred years of the dynasty were peaceful. The emphasis the new dynasty gave Confucianism led to the repression of Buddhism, the closing of temples, and the removal of monks from positions of political importance. It also created an intellectual ferment that was to come to a boil in the reign of King Sejong, the fourth king of the dynasty, who reigned from 1419 to 1450.

Stabilization of the country had given scholars more freedom from the duties of government and more time for study. Impressive advances were being made. By 1403 books had been printed using movable metal type, though there is good reason to believe Koreans knew of the use of movable type as early as 1234, nearly fifty years before Gutenberg developed movable type printing in Europe. King Sejong brought the best minds of the country together. During his rule, rain gauges were invented and systematic records kept of rainfall; an astronomical office was established which developed many new devices and kept records of eclipses and other related phenomena; a careful geographical survey of the peninsula was made. But perhaps the most dramatic of all was the creation of an alphabet for the writing of Korean.

By historical accident the Chinese writing system had come to be used in Korea. Though an attempt had been made during the Silla period to adopt the Chinese character to the Korean language, the resulting system was too awkward for general use and most writing continued to be done in Chinese while Korean was the spoken language. King Sejong felt the need for a practical way of writing Korean, and after years of study by a group of scholars the twenty-eight letter Korean alphabet was completed in the 1440s and many books were quickly published in the new alphabet.

After King Sejong's reign the political situation began a decline. Factions grew up around the court, each fighting for personal advantage. Many of the scholars who had been drawn into government service in Sejong's time were either in disfavor or had returned to their homes in the countryside to pursue their studies undisturbed by the troubles in the capital. An increasing number of scholars turned away from the government to the pursuit of knowledge.

This scattering of the scholars led to the growth of many private schools. Here Confucianism was taught and scholars continued their speculations. These schools, which had no connection with the official government schools that trained young scholars preparing for the examinations, produced some of the most brilliant scholars Korea had ever seen. Many of the young men trained there were to take the government examinations and rise in the ranks of able civil servants.

But despite the flourishing of scholarship in the years following Sejong's reign, the factional struggles that shook the court left Korea badly prepared to meet the attack of the next major foreign aggressor, Japan.

In 1592, the Japanese shogun, Toyotomi Hideyoshi, ordered his forces into Korea as the first step toward the conquest of China. Thousands of Japanese boats landed at Pusan and the armies rushed up the peninsula toward Seoul. The Koreans put up hardly any defense. They were unprepared for war, their leaders were incompetent, and they were facing a Japanese army equipped with new weapons which European traders had only recently taught the Japanese how to make.

Yet while they were losing on land the Koreans managed to take control of the sea. Admiral Yi Sun-sin, one of the great Korean heroes, utilizing a technical knowledge and skill that were highly advanced for the time, had prepared for just this sort of emergency. His famous "turtle ships," so called because they were armored and shaped like turtles, were invulnerable to attack by the usual methods. They were able to sail right into the Japanese fleet, wreaking destruction wherever they went. As a result the Japanese land armies were cut off from supplies and reinforcements from Japan.

In the meantime, the king had turned to Ming China for help, and a Chinese army moved in, aiding the Koreans to recapture key positions. Battle morale was improved, and small guerrilla bands were formed which scored heavily against the Japanese. By the end of 1593 the Japanese were pocketed in a small area in the south; the king had returned to Seoul, and an informal truce was in effect.

This truce extended for nearly four years. Yet despite the critical situation, the factional struggles within the Korean court went on, and even the hero of the war, Admiral Yi Sun-sin, fell victim and was removed from his command.

In the beginning of 1597 the truce ended, and the Japanese launched another invasion fleet. This threat brought quick reaction. Admiral Yi was reinstated, though not in time to prevent the landing of the Japanese fleet. Ming China again was asked for aid.

This time things did not go so well for the Japanese, and they were forced back by the combined armies of China and Korea. In 1598 Hideyoshi died; the Japanese armies were bottled up at the southern tip of the peninsula and retreated to their boats to set sail for Japan. But Admiral Yi Sun-sin was waiting, and though he was killed in the battle, he took full revenge upon the retreating Japanese fleet.

During the course of the war all the major Korean cities had been occupied by the Japanese armies. Many had been burned as well as looted, and the material drain on the people was immense—not only to supply an army, but to meet the demands of the large Chinese force that came to their aid.

The secret gardens of the Changdŏk Palace in Seoul, landscaped in 1623.

As Korea began to recover from the Japanese invasion a new threat was growing to the north. A small Manchurian group, the Manchus, had grown strong enough to threaten Ming China. In 1619 the Ming emperor asked the Koreans for help against the Manchus, and a Korean army was sent, only to be turned back in defeat. In 1627 the Manchus invaded Korea. The Korean army was defeated and the people suffered greatly. However, even then the court refused to recognize the inevitable rise of the Manchu power and continued to support Ming. In 1636 the Manchu invaded again, causing even more destruction on the peninsula and finally forcing the capitulation of the court. Even after the Manchu had established themselves in the Chinese capital in 1644 as the Ching dynasty, there still remained a hard core of resistance among the Koreans. To them the Ming were still the real rulers of China.

Partially as a result of the terrible destruction brought to Korea by attacks from the outside, the peninsula entered into a period of strict isolation from the outside world. Ports were closed, and the only contacts were made by the official delegations to Peking or Japan, or an occasional diplomatic mission to another country. Korea had had enough of outsiders. For over two hundred years she was indeed the "hermit nation."

The court continued to be torn by factional strife during most of this period, weakening internal administration. Intellectual life cut off from outside stimulation began to stagnate. But not all new ideas could be cut off. The seventeenth century saw the introduction of gunpowder, more modern weapons, telescopes, clocks, and maps from Ming China, together with books on astronomy, geography, and the sciences, which served as an introduction to what the Chinese of the time knew of Western developments. By the second half of the eighteenth century ideas from the West, including Roman Catholic teaching, had been carried into the country by members of the annual mission to the Chinese court.

These ideas helped to stimulate the work of a group called the Sirhakp'a, made up of scholars outside the government service, who began to approach all fields of learning with their new ideas. The existing social order was criticized. All aspects of life in Korea were investigated and reevaluated, resulting in works on economics, history, geography, and agriculture. But these men on the whole were in political opposition to those who controlled the court. The practical results of their work were limited, though one of them, Pak Ch'i-wŏn, did achieve some effect by a series of satirical stories written in Chinese which criticized the existing order of things on the basis of these new ideas. The court ordered him to stop writing in his particular style of Chinese on the grounds that it was not approved by the scholars. It was clear, however, that the order was aimed at the stories themselves—the court was not ready to allow this sort of open criticism.

A Korean who had accompanied one of the annual missions to Peking and had been baptized into the Catholic church began to convert others to the new religion after his return to Korea. Catholicism spread and by 1791 had become important enough to lead to a prohibition of it and to the burning of Western books. Any contact with the West was forbidden, and religion was in no way exempted.

Despite persecutions and a wholesale massacre of Catholics in 1801, interest in the foreign religion continued to grow. From 1836 to 1839, French missionaries worked in Korea, even though no foreigners were supposed to enter the country. In 1839 Catholicism was proscribed again; believers were executed in great numbers, and with them the French missionaries.

As Korea became more and more aware of the pressures of the Western world upon the Orient, she increased her determination to have nothing to do with that world. She had seen China forced to open her doors to the West in 1842, and Japan made to follow in 1854. On the whole she did not approve of what she had seen. But Catholicism and Western books, and even Western priests, had slipped in despite the attempts of the court to suppress them.

The internal situation continued to deteriorate. At the end of the eighteenth century and the beginning of the nineteenth, strong individuals and families, particularly the Kim family, were granted extraordinary powers by the king. Since they were not a part of the regular government structure, they could easily turn their power to their own advantage, exploiting the people for their own personal gain. Greed and corruption on the part of government officials was weakening the court. There were increasing instances of resistance to the government in rural areas, and in 1811 these were organized into an extensive rebellion. It was short-lived, but it required a major effort on the part of the government to put it down.

In the following years there were more and more outbreaks of dissatisfaction in rural areas. This feeling was to be synthesized with the traditionalist fears of foreign encroachment by Ch'oe Che-u, who founded a new nationalistic religion in 1860, the year Lincoln was elected president of the United States. Ch'oe Che-u, who himself belonged to the upper ruling class, by his own account had wandered over the countryside for more than twenty years searching for a way to save mankind. When he was thirty-seven God spoke to him and showed him a "new way" to save the people which he formulated into a new religion.

This new religion was called Tonghak (Eastern Learning) by its founder to distinguish it, both in purpose and kind, from Sŏhak (Western Learning), the name by which Catholicism had come to be known. Tonghak did not concern itself with an afterlife. It stressed that heaven would be created here on earth when present evil and corruption were eliminated. Widely popular among the suffering people, it soon began to cause serious concern on the part of the government as it led to organized uprisings around the country. Its followers were persecuted in 1863, and in the following year its founder was sentenced to death. But, though the movement was banned, Tonghak, like Catholicism and foreign learning, continued in Korea, and still remains today under the name of Ch'ŏndogyo.

In 1864 a new king was enthroned, Kojong, whose reign was to span the most eventful days of the declining dynasty. He was still a child, and his father assumed the power of the throne as prince regent, known in Korean as the Taewŏngun. The Taewŏngun was a complex man, seen by some as a devil, by others as a savior. He assumed his power at a time when the corruption of the court was at its worst. The power of the king was at a low ebb; effective power was in the hands of the all-powerful Kim family. The Taewŏngun did all he could to remedy this situation and reaffirm royal authority. One way of doing this was to marry King Kojong to a member of the powerful Min family, thus effectively keeping the Kims away from direct contact with the royal household. But despite the Taewŏngun's efforts to strengthen the internal administration he was a violent isolationist and strongly against foreign contacts with any nation other than China.

The continual isolationism of the court was severely tested by internal pressures: the persistence of the Catholic fathers and believers, and the reaching out for new Western knowledge by the members of the Sirhakp'a. With the year 1866 the world powers began to exert pressures from outside.

Early in 1866 a Russian gunboat anchored off a northeastern port, requesting Korea to establish trade relations with czarist Russia. Shortly after this, nine of twelve disguised French Catholic priests who had been proselytizing in the country were exposed and executed by order of the Taewŏngun. This led to an armed attack on the island of Kanghwa by a French fleet. The French were beaten back.

In the same year an American ship, the *General Sherman*, sailed up the Taedong River to P'yŏngyang where it ran aground. The Koreans mistook the nonviolent intentions of the crew, as the crew apparently did those of the Koreans, and in the following battle all the Americans were killed. When an American gunboat arrived to inquire about the fate of the ship the Americans were simply told to go away, which they did. In the spring of 1871, another American expedition landed on Kanghwa Island. It resulted in a fight leading to the deaths of hundreds of people, among them three Americans.

None of these expeditions reduced the confidence of the Kore-

Artist's sketch of Seoul around 1876, before Korea was opened to the West.

ans in their ability to defend themselves against the power of the Western nations. They had, after all, come out on top in all encounters, and they found no good reason to hold Westerners in high regard. But Korea's isolation was soon to come to an end.

In 1872 the Japanese sent to the Korean court an envoy who managed to open the eyes of some, including Queen Min, to the importance of international diplomacy, even though the Taewŏn-gun frustrated all attempts at establishing diplomatic relations with Japan. However, when a Japanese ship was fired upon by the Koreans, Japan made an issue of the incident, and in 1876 sent a military force. Rather than fight, however, the Japanese chose to negotiate, and in February, 1876 a treaty was ratified between Korea and Japan that marked Korea's emergence from her period of isolation.

6

Chosŏn: The Meeting with the West

The treaty with Japan was soon to be followed by others: with the United States in 1882; the United Kingdom and Germany, 1883; Italy and Russia, 1884; France, 1886; and Austria, 1892. But opening her doors to the world did not solve the problems that plagued Korea. The people were suffering from the corruption and greed of their own officials. The government was weak and faction-ridden. The rulers had little skill in international diplomacy, having left all diplomatic relations in the recent past in the hands of China. As a result they let their country become a pawn in the international power struggle in East Asia.

After over two hundred years of isolation the sight of the outside world was a great and exciting thing to those Koreans who were made aware of it. Missions were sent by the government to China and Japan in 1880 to see what they could learn from the modernization taking place in those countries. The members of the missions were deeply impressed by their journeys. As diplomatic relations were established with Western nations more Koreans traveled farther, to the United States, Europe, and Russia, and brought back stories of what they had seen and learned. A small, but steadily growing, progressive group felt that Korea too, must join the modern world, but there also remained strong conservative elements in the court that resisted change.

China urged that the Koreans establish diplomatic relations with Western powers as a way of countering the growing Japanese power on the peninsula and strengthening China's own. The power struggle within the Korean court became, for the time at least, a contest between pro-Chinese and pro-Japanese elements that relied on the strength and prestige of their outside backers, China and Japan, to help keep them in power.

To remain in power required more than the backing of outside forces. The king, despite the corruption and declining power of his government, remained an absolute monarch. Only those who gained his favor could expect the royal seal of approval on their plans. Action within the court was not obtained by well-reasoned arguments and careful planning; it was done only through convincing the king himself that he should approve of it.

The main street of Seoul in 1882.

Both King Kojong and Queen Min were rulers who had the best interests of their country at heart. The queen was the more powerful personality, and as long as she lived she had a strong influence upon the king. It was her influence, along with the powerful backing of the Min family, that had allowed the king to take over full control of his throne and force the Taewŏngun into the background. She had been one of the first convinced of the desirability of a treaty with Japan. The Taewŏngun kept official silence, but it was clear he was waiting for the opportunity, which eventually came, to reassert his dominance over King Kojong, who, pleasant and sincere as he might have been, had little of the insight and personal leadership required to carry his country through such troubled years.

In 1881 reforms were introduced in the military system when a Japanese military officer was brought in to train a new army along Western lines. This created a great deal of dissension in the old-line army. The next year, making a complaint over late payment of grain rations, the old army launched a revolt. Soldiers marched in the streets, joined by many who had their own grievances against the way things were going at court, and attacked the government. The queen was forced to flee, leaving the Taewŏngun in virtual control. After killing the Japanese army officer who was training the troops, the soldiers directed their attack on the Japanese legation, forcing the Japanese minister and his staff to flee. The Chinese took this as an opportunity to regain their position of supremacy in Korea, and sent troops accompanied by a high ranking diplomat to help reestablish order. The Taewŏngun, who had clearly had a hand in the uprising, was shipped off to China, and when things had settled down, Queen Min, who was generally thought to have been killed in the turmoil, emerged from her sanctuary in the countryside.

There was a group of young reformers around the court who felt that Japan was the force for modernization and favored her in the power struggle. In 1884 they established a reform cabinet by military coup—aided by soldiers who were in Seoul. Leaders of the old cabinet were killed; the king was abducted and placed under armed Japanese guard. The group proclaimed an ambitious program of reform, and it looked for the moment as if the old rule had been broken. However, China was quick to act, especially since there was little public support for the reformers. She moved her troops in, and three days after the reforms had been announced the Japanese were in flight again; the king and queen were back on the throne.

The China-Japan power struggle came to a head in 1894. Although they had been banned, the Tonghak organized a revolt against the government, stimulated in part by the terrible conditions in the countryside, in part by a distrust of growing foreign influence on the government. Therefore, the Korean government asked China for aid in putting down the revolt. By sending in their troops, the Chinese in effect broke an agreement with Japan which had said that neither party would do this without informing the other. The Japanese sent their troops in as well, and war broke out between Japan and China. Japan easily defeated the Chinese.

The Japanese were in firm control on the peninsula, and during the war, in 1894, forced a series of modernization reforms upon the Korean court. By this time both King Kojong and Queen Min had had enough of the Chinese-Japanese struggle for control, for it seemed clear that Japan was simply trying to gain the position in Seoul that China had held before. In the middle of such trying events they turned to Russia, the third power whose interests in the peninsula were strong, but which at the time seemed trustworthy, in the hopes that she would serve to counterbalance the power of Japan. When a plot was uncovered in which the Japanese had planned to depose the queen in order to gain more control over the king, the turn to Russia for protection was inevitable. In a last desperate move aimed at securing the Japanese position in Korea, a group of Japanese attacked the royal palace, murdered the queen, and forced the frightened king to appoint a pro-Japanese cabinet.

The new cabinet then proceeded to push through the reforms of 1894. Armed defiance resulted in the countryside, and the better part of the government troops had to be dispatched to suppress it. These signs of popular aversion to Japanese power did not escape the Russian minister in Seoul. He carefully arranged for the arrival of an embassy guard of one hundred Russian soldiers, and then managed to have the Korean king take refuge in the Russian embassy. The pro-Russian and anti-Japanese elements in the country took full advantage of this situation to wipe out their opposition. When the king left the Russian embassy for his own palace on February 20, 1897, Russia's position on the peninsula was strong.

During this period a number of concessions had been granted to foreign powers. Russia, of course, took full advantage of being the king's protector. She gained valuable lumbering rights along the northern Korean border, mining rights in the interior, the right to supervise the military training of Korea's army, and, of major importance, the right to handle the finances of the Korean government. At the same time the United States demanded, and received, concessions for a Seoul-Inch'ŏn railroad, for gold mining in the interior, and for a streetcar line in Seoul. Concessions were granted to Japan for a Pusan-Seoul railroad, and gold mining also; to Britain and Germany for gold mining; and to France for a railroad from Seoul to the northwest border of Korea.

All of this stirred up a good deal of unrest among the intellectuals who were growing more and more concerned over the government's lack of initiative and constant reliance on outside help. In 1896 a group of these men, some of whom had been educated in the United States, had banded together in the Independence Club, and they gave Korea her first modern newspaper, the *Independence News*. They criticized the government for selling out to foreign powers, and emphasized the spirit of freedom, civil rights, and national independence. Although the Independence Club existed for only a year it was the first example of a democratic organization at work in Korea. It served as a training ground for many young political leaders. One of these was Syngman Rhee, who was to become better known as the first president of the Republic of Korea after World War II.

In 1897 King Kojong took the title of emperor, a move that obviously was an attempt to equalize Korea's position with that of the three great powers around her, China, Japan, and Russia. China and Japan had emperors, and in the past the Korean king had been subordinate to the Chinese emperor. Now he assumed equal status, in title at least.

The following seven years were a relatively quiet period politically. Russia and Japan continued to vie for power on the peninsula, and foreign interests in Korea expanded. New ports were opened to trade, telegraphic communications were established, and an electric company began providing power to Seoul; the railway between Seoul and Inch'ŏn began operations, and in 1903 the first telephones came into use. Schools and hospitals were opened. The Protestant missionaries who had been active since the opening of Korea in 1882 expanded their work greatly in one of the most successful undertakings in the history of Christian missions.

Then in 1904 Japan broke off diplomatic relations with Russia and, without a formal declaration of war, launched an attack on

Seoul around the turn of the century.

Russia. Most of the battles were fought outside Korean territory, but Korea was forced into the position of being Japan's ally. Japan won the war, and in the flush of victory began to press her advantage in Korea.

In 1905 an agreement with Japan was signed, under strong Japanese pressure, which established Korea as a Japanese protectorate, giving the Japanese resident-general complete power in directing Korean foreign relations, which were to be carried on through Tokyo. In fact, his powers reached into all fields of Korean governmental activity. The signing of the treaty was kept secret for some time, but as soon as the news became public there were nationwide protests. Some high court officials committed suicide in protest in front of the palace gates. In 1906 there were several provincial revolts, but the Japanese used troops to put them down.

In 1906 all Korean foreign diplomatic missions were closed, and all foreign diplomatic missions in Korea withdrew in tacit acceptance of the Japanese right to control the peninsula. In 1907 the Korean emperor made his last move in the fight for Korean freedom from Japan. He secretly dispatched a delegation to the Second International Peace Conference at the Hague to plead Korea's cause. It met with no success.

The same year the emperor was forced to abdicate in favor of the crown prince, who the Japanese felt would be more easily controlled. In August, 1910, a treaty of annexation was signed. Korea was incorporated into the Japanese empire. The Chosŏn kingdom, founded by Yi Sŏng-gye one hundred years before the discovery of America, came to an end.

7

Korea in Our Century

From 1910 to 1945 Korea remained a colony of Japan. This was a bitter experience. A small but growing progressive movement had been developing at the end of the Yi dynasty, with a vision of a modernized Korea taking her place as an equal among the nations of the world. With Japanese annexation in 1910 these hopes were cut short. A Japanese government-general was established, and for the next thirty-five years Korea was to be known as Chosen, the Japanese pronunciation of Chosŏn.

Although Japan had been the most successful Asian nation in adapting Western ideas and technology to her modernization, Koreans tended to look upon her with condescension. They had never valued the civilization of the islands, and had looked upon the Japanese as barbarians. Yet all power was now to be in the hands of the Japanese; the loyalty of the Koreans was to be directed toward the Japanese emperor. There was no Korean emperor; the Korean nation no longer existed.

The stated aim of the Japanese in Korea was no less than the complete assimilation of a great and ancient nation and culture. During the first ten years, their rule was highly oppressive. Small local Korean "armies" offered armed resistance but were forced to retreat to Manchuria by the overwhelming strength of the

Japanese. Quick to gain control of land and the fledgling Korean industries, the Japanese developed transportation, fisheries, and communications, and exploited natural resources such as minerals and forests.

When the Japanese pointed with pride to their accomplishments on the peninsula, the Koreans asked: At what cost? What price do we Koreans have to pay to keep our rice pots filled? As one young Korean historian put it, writing in the 1920s: "To the Koreans mountains are not property to be bought and sold. Mountains are the precious ornaments of our land. They are where we exercise our minds and bodies; they are a symbol of the beliefs and ideals informing men and girls, individuals and communities, the life of now and the life of ideals. . . . Our Korean people as yet cannot think of filling their rice pots by selling them." But in actuality they had no choice. The Japanese had taken the mountains and everything else besides.

On March 1, 1919 there were peaceful demonstrations in Seoul demanding independence from Japan; within a few days the whole peninsula was in turmoil. The outburst, known as the March First Independence Movement, was no accidental firing of mob violence. It had been well planned. On March 1, a group of thirty prominent Koreans met around noon in a Seoul restaurant. They sent the governor-general a declaration of independence which they had signed, as had three others who were not present. Then they called the Japanese police, explaining what they had done, and waited. By the time the police arrived to arrest them the streets were lined with people cheering them off on their way to jail.

The Korean people were well aware of what was happening. By mid-afternoon, special messengers had read the declaration of independence aloud in towns and villages all over the country. Peaceful demonstrations were held across the nation.

The timing of the March First Independence Movement was influenced by two events. The former Korean emperor had died and his funeral was scheduled for March 3. Common report had it that he had been poisoned by the Japanese, and resentment was at a boiling point. At the same time, President Wilson's doctrine of self-determination for subjugated nations was beginning to be understood. Driven by this hope, a group of Korean students in Tokyo had published in February, 1919 a statement demanding Korea's independence from Japan. By the first of March, plans had been made to reinforce this demand in Korea by means of peaceful demonstrations and the presentation of the Declaration of Independence to the governor-general.

The demonstrations were peaceful, but the Japanese power retaliated in full force. There were wholesale imprisonments, open floggings, and brutal killings of demonstrators.

Despite tight censorship in Korea, the news spread, and soon the outside world was registering horror at the extent of Japanese brutalities. Pressures from world opinion demanded a change. In August, 1919, the governor-general was replaced.

Japanese power in the peninsula was not broken. But during the next decade the administration of that power was to be a little less severe. Japan had been forced to come to terms with the power of Korean national feeling.

But, while things were somewhat better for the next fifteen years, they were not good. In 1926 there were student uprisings against the Japanese and again in 1928. In 1929 nationwide anti-Japanese demonstrations occurred. In 1931, as Japan moved into Manchuria and toward war with China, controls became more rigid, and this continued during the 1930s. In 1938 the use of the Korean language in the schools was banned along with the teaching of Korean history. In 1940 Koreans were ordered to adopt Japanese names. In the same year the two remaining Korean-language newspapers were suspended and restrictions on all publications in Korean became most severe.

Korea had become an integral part of the Japanese war machine, and after the attack on Pearl Harbor in December of 1941 and the entry of the United States into the war Koreans were drafted into the Japanese army. Korea was stripped of anything that could be used to further the war effort: manpower went to factories in Japan, forests were leveled, even the iron pipes of the Seoul water system went to the iron-hungry blast furnaces.

Korea was freed from thirty-five years of Japanese rule when Japan surrendered in August, 1945. Her independence had been promised at the Cairo Conference, where China, England, Russia, and the United States met in 1943, and that promise had been reaffirmed in the Potsdam Declaration of 1945 by China, England, and the United States.

But liberation from Japanese rule again found Korea caught up in a power struggle. This time it was the "cold war" between the Soviet Union and the West. After the shouting and celebrations had died down, it soon became clear that creation of a unified and independent Korea was to be no easy task.

The Soviet Union had entered the war in the Pacific shortly before the Japanese surrender in 1945. At the Potsdam Conference it was decided that to facilitate accepting the Japanese surrender in Korea, Soviet forces would come as far south as the 38th parallel, and the American forces would come up from the south and meet them there. The result was a Korea divided at the middle.

As soon as the Japanese surrender was official, Korean leaders all over the country moved to set up what was called the Preparatory Association for Establishing the Nation. Administrative units were set up from the lowest to the highest levels to assure the continuance of civil order with the end of Japanese power.

In the north the Soviet forces came into Korea accompanied by thousands of highly trained Koreans who had lived in Siberian Russia during the Japanese occupation, some of whom had served in the Soviet armies during the Second World War, and most of whom were devoted to the cause of world communism. The American forces were accompanied by few Koreans and almost no interpreters. These Koreans were mainly those who had carried on the anti-Japanese struggle in the United States, and they had been out of contact with Korea for years. As a result of these differences in personnel, the two occupying forces were to treat the local Korean organization in very different ways.

The Soviet forces in the north did not often involve themselves directly in political developments. They left this up to their Russian-trained Korean fellows. Soon control of the Preparatory Association was in the hands of Koreans sympathetic to communism.

On the other hand, the United States forces set up a military government in the south. Activities such as those of the Preparatory Association aimed at the setting up of a Korean government were banned by the end of 1945. To many in South Korea it seemed as if they had simply exchanged one foreign rule for another. And to make the situation worse, their country was now divided.

It soon became apparent that no local solution of the problem of division was possible. Despite the efforts of the Soviet Union, the United States, and Britain in setting up a joint commission to work out the problems of unification, the situation was still dead-locked in 1947 when the United States felt it necessary to place the Korean question before the second session of the United Nations General Assembly. A United Nations Temporary Commission for Korea was set up to supervise general elections over the whole of the peninsula. When the commission tried to carry out the planned elections it found itself barred from the Russian-occupied zone in the north.

In 1948 general elections under United Nations supervision were carried out in the south only. The party led by Syngman Rhee—a man who had devoted his life to the cause of Korean independence from Japan, but who had spent most of the first forty years of this century in the United States and the West—won the elections after a period of bitter fighting among the many political groups seeking power. He was the first president of the Republic of Korea. This government was recognized by the United Nations as the only legitimate government of all Korea.

Events began to move rapidly. The Korean Democratic People's Republic was set up in the north with its capital at P'yŏng-yang, and the division of Korea was complete. This government was led by Kim Il Sung, a Korean Communist general who had led a guerrilla army in Manchuria during the 1930s. By 1950 most hopes for peaceful unification of the country under one government had been lost. On June 25, 1950, war broke out along the 38th parallel.

The North Korean forces advanced rapidly, taking Seoul and bottling up the South Korean forces in the area around Pusan on the southern tip of the peninsula. It was at this point that President Truman ordered American forces into Korea to assist the South Korean army.

On June 27, the United Nations recommended that its members support the South Koreans against the aggression from the north. The United Nations Command was set up in Korea in July, and, as the war progressed, the forces of sixteen nations were fighting in Korea. Seven other nations sent hospital ships, field hospitals, and other assistance.

The war continued up and down the length of the peninsula for over two years. After the formation of the United Nations

Refugees fleeing south during the Korean War.

Command in July, 1950, the North Korean forces were slowly pushed north until at the end of October, United Nations forces were at the Yalu River, the Manchurian border.

At this point troops from mainland China entered the war, again forcing a retreat south of Seoul by the South Korean and United Nations forces. By the end of March, 1951, the South Korean and United Nations troops had forced their way back to the 38th parallel. Two months later, a fairly stable battle line had been established in the general area of the parallel. Truce talks began in July, 1951.

Seoul just after the war.

Visitors mill around outside a guarded meeting hall at Panmunjŏm, site of the armistice meetings.

After two years of negotiations an armistice agreement was finally reached. Peace of a sort came to Korea when it was signed on July 27, 1953. A military demarcation line was established along the front where fighting had been taking place during the long months of negotiation. A distance of two kilometers on each side of this line was designated a kind of no-man's-land, known as the Demilitarized Zone or DMZ.

The years that followed were not easy ones. There was the agonizing realization that the division of the country was to continue. Both north and south were faced with the problems of rebuilding out of the destruction of war and somehow moving their economies forward to eliminate the hunger and poverty that could only be alleviated partially and temporarily by outside aid.

8

The Republic of Korea

The Republic of Korea (ROK) was created on May 10, 1948. A national assembly was elected which approved a constitutional government patterned on that of the United States was executive, legislative, and judicial branches. On August 15, 1948, General MacArthur, as commander of United States forces in the Far East, turned over the United States military government in Korea to the first president of the independent ROK, Syngman Rhee.

Syngman Rhee was a remarkable individual. In the 1890s he had been a junior member of the Independence Club and active in efforts to liberalize the Korean monarchy. Imprisoned and tortured, after release he made his way to Japan, Hawaii, and eventually the United States. He attended several colleges, and after completing study at Princeton where he took some of his graduate work under Woodrow Wilson, he returned to Korea as a YMCA worker. Like many of the South Korean political leaders he was a Christian. Soon after the annexation he left Korea again for Hawaii.

In his years of exile Rhee worked continuously in the cause of Korean independence. He was Washington representative for the Korean government-in-exile, based in China, during the 1930s and 1940s. In his earlier attempts to bring the Korean situation to world attention he had spent time in Europe hoping to influence the League of Nations. While there he married an Austrian. When he returned to Korea in 1945 at the end of the Pacific war—after living abroad for the greater part of forty years—he was already past seventy.

Syngman Rhee created intense loyalties and violent opposition. He was careful not to allow an opposition politician to grow too strong; he would even cut down members of his own party if he felt they were gaining too much popularity. His followers resorted to political assassination at times, and have been accused of staging attempts upon the lives of members of their own party in order to gain popular support for strong government actions which would in the end serve to suppress democratic processes and civil liberties.

The older Rhee grew, the more isolated he became from the real political needs of the ROK. He was carefully isolated by a small group of "insiders" who surrounded him and then used their prestige and power for personal gain. Graft and corruption were common; many pressing needs of the nation were being neglected.

Rhee's was a "strongman" government. When conflicts occurred among the three branches, in times of crisis the executive most often emerged with the real power. Rhee, a skillful and often ruthless politician, forced through several constitutional amendments strengthening presidential powers, yet managed to preserve the appearance of respecting democratic processes and organizations.

It is easy to fault this old man: he remained violently anti-Japanese to the end, leaving no chance of a Korean rapprochement with Japan while he was in power. He was conservative, politically and personally, subject to the common human failing of labeling those with whom he disagreed with the most opprobrious terms in his vocabulary—Communist, fellow-traveler—without regard to the truth of the matter. He was vulnerable to sycophants and old friends. But in time of great crises, the years of the Korean War, he served as a popular rallying point for the defense of the south. He stood as the first titular and real head of well over half the Korean population after forty years of colonial rule. He was symbol and power. Certainly he was heir to many human shortcomings; certainly he could have been called to task for the obvious gap between what he said should and would be done and what in actuality resulted. But who cannot? It is a measure of the man that his fall was great. Only those who venture into high places may fall far. Syngman Rhee continued as president of the ROK until his government was overthrown by student rioting in April, 1960.

In the elections of 1958 an opposition candidate defeated Rhee's chosen running mate. Rhee's party lost heavily in the legislative races. The war was over and the external threat did not seem so immediate. Army officers, many of them American-trained, hardened and tested by the rigors of the battlefield, were beginning to take an interest in politics. They found the prevalent graft in government distasteful, especially when it affected the procurement of adequate materiel and supplies for the military. The army and the civilian population were disgusted and bitter over the high-handed tactics of the national police, many of whom were holdovers from the days of the Japanese occupation. They had changed their masters, but not their trade or methods.

By the time of the 1960 elections the forces of the opposition, strongly supported by students and intellectuals, had gained considerable strength. Though Rhee was able to retain his popularity in the rural areas, he had never been greatly popular in the urban centers. Those closest to him were determined their party would not show losses like those of the previous election. They went to all extremes to suppress the opposition and rig the election to secure a strong vote for Rhee's party. The police were enlisted to help suppress the opposition and their tactics were harsh. When the corpse of a student, a victim of the police, was found floating in the harbor of a southern port there was a nationwide outcry.

The subsequent overwhelming, and unbelievable, victory by Rhee's party at the polls brought on a crisis. College and high school students in Seoul marched out in protest on April 19, 1960. Police reaction was predictable. One hundred twenty-five of the

Fishing village in the Republic of Korea.

demonstrating students were shot down. Students took to the streets en masse supplemented by their professors. Arms linked, they marched down the streets protesting the elections and police brutality. Martial law was declared.

But many army leaders sympathized with the demonstrators and were unwilling to move against them. They even went so far as to commend as just the demands of university professors that certain key officials in all three branches of the government resign. On top of this, President Rhee was faced with a note from the U.S. State Department expressing strong opposition to the harsh measures which had been employed. On April 22, 1960, Syngman Rhee resigned and left Korea for the last time, to live out his life in Hawaii. Upon his death a few years later his body was returned to Seoul and given a state funeral, perhaps in recognition of the fact that sometimes the good that men do may indeed live after them.

Upon Syngman Rhee's voluntary exile to Hawaii, a caretaker government took over until elections could be held. It was a period of considerable excitement and anticipation. The police were, temporarily at least, discredited and restrained. The students, intellectuals, and all those who had joined in the movement against the government were elated. Restrictions on the press, movies, and assembly were lifted.

In July, 1960, elections were held. A parliamentary form of government was established with Yun Posun as titular president and John M. Chang as premier and actual head of state. One recalls the brief months of the Chang government with pleasure despite the presence of obvious political storm warnings. There was unprecedented gaiety and spontaneity in everyday life even though actual living conditions did not get better, and in fact became worse. Position in government only too often still suggested, and became, a means to graft, and corruption spread throughout the political parties. John Chang was never able to bring together a working majority in his legislature and so was, in many ways, ineffectual as a leader.

The police had been so thoroughly discredited that even newly organized, and with full government support, they were incapable of maintaining civil order. Freedom of the press became extended to irresponsible action by the press. For the first time since 1948 there was open talk of reconciliation with the north, rank heresy in Rhee days. There were protest demonstrations everywhere. The economy was faltering badly, inflation was severe; little was done though much was said about a new agricultural program; a black market, reminiscent of the days shortly after the Korean War, flourished in PX and other American army goods. And leaders in the armed forces found their positions threatened by proposed cutbacks in the military budget.

In the early morning hours of May 16, 1961, a group of Korean soldiers took control of the government buildings, the radio stations, and the city of Seoul in a bloodless coup. The gaiety ended, and the streets of the city were lined with impassive faces watching the passing military leaders. After years of repressions and hopes and repressions and hopes rekindled, many Koreans could feel only emotional exhaustion and submission to fate.

Under the military, the governing body was called the Supreme Council for National Reconstruction. It consisted of thirty-two military officers headed by the commander-in-chief of the army. President Yun Posun was retained in office to give some semblance of constitutional continuity, while John M. Chang and his cabinet were arrested on charges of corruption. The Supreme Council quickly set about instituting changes in the constitution and the administration.

Not too many weeks passed before open signs of strain appeared within the Supreme Council, and soon the commander-in-chief was forced to resign. In his place the real leader of the coup took over. Major General Park Chung Hee, less well known to Western or even Korean observers than many of the other officers, proved to be the strongman of the military government.

The military government moved toward making immediate reforms in what they felt were major problem areas. They struck out first at graft and political corruption. All political activities were suspended; men who had amassed large fortunes through corrupt or illegal means were forced to donate large sums to national economic projects or to pay heavy fines. An immediate clampdown upon the press was intended ostensibly to stop the publication of "irresponsible papers," but actually amounted to censorship. Many political appointees were removed and replaced by military officers or by civilian specialists. In general there was an effort to create a more efficient and better-disciplined government—a government that would perhaps, operate more like the military. There was also a promise that as soon as effective reforms could be carried out, probably in two years, and a new constitution could be drafted and approved by the people, elections would be held for a civilian government.

The Supreme Council, zealous for reform, seemed to think the country could be run like an army. But they soon collided with the hard fact that the needs of civilians, and the economic and political problems of running a country, require solutions very different from simple military orders or decrees. A five-year plan had been drawn up, but it did not work out so well in practice as it did on paper. The government was faced with a growing population, a static economy, and passive resistance on the part of some civilian leaders that made much of their planning ineffectual or effectually slowed it down.

In the meantime, the question of the legality of the government became a major issue. Although the military leaders had been able to persuade President Yun Posun to give some appearance of legality by remaining in office, he soon resigned. General Park was appointed acting president. It became imperative to hold to the promise of elections, though General Park was hesitant, feeling very unsure of his political strength. However, the military officers doffed their uniforms and stood for election as civilians. There were three viable presidential candidates.

Park Chung Hee as a civilian won by a small margin. There was no reason to question the fairness of the elections. The presidential election was followed by elections for the legislature, and again President Park's Democratic-Republican party carried a majority. The Republic of Korea was once again under civilian rule.

Park Chung Hee's background and preparation for national leadership were as different as possible from those of Syngman Rhee. He was born in southeastern Korea without any of the aristocratic credentials that Rhee carried. His formal education stopped with high school. From there he was drafted into the Japanese army and chosen for officer training in the Japanese military academy in Manchuria. During World War II he was an officer in the Japanese army. With the liberation of Korea he entered the Korean military and advanced rapidly. As a ROK colonel he was sentenced to death on charges of being involved in the Communist-inspired Yosu revolt of army forces in 1948. He was ultimately cleared and pardoned by Syngman Rhee. During the Korean War he served in various capacities.

Though Park has had some military training in the United States, he has never cultivated associations with American officers. There is little doubt that, while President Park fully realizes the extent to which the ROK is dependent upon U.S. and other foreign aid, he is an independent, if not highly original thinker, and resents any implication of outside influence. For him it is most important that Koreans find Korean solutions to Korean problems, though in doing so they may lean heavily upon outside models. He is firmly convinced that the failure of past ROK governments has been due to the Koreans' lack of experience in democratic government, and the underlying idea of all his governmental reforms and programs has been to create a situation in which democratic ideas and methods can be made to develop and work in a Korean way.

He is presently serving his fourth term as president of the Republic of Korea, reelected in December, 1972, to a six-year term under the provisions of a new constitution ratified by a national referendum in November. The constitution allows the president to take emergency measures whenever he wants to impose more nearly complete control over South Korea. It has also weakened the powers of the parliament and changed the method of selecting the presidents, from a popular vote to voting by members of a special body. Perhaps the most basic problem of Park's years in office has been that of developing in the Korean people a sense of trust in the national government. How far he has succeeded remains to be seen; despite strong measures taken to control graft and corruption, several major scandals have rocked the Park government.

On the positive side, during Park Chung Hee's years as president the Korean government has managed to establish friendly relations with Japan, has encouraged foreign investment in Korea, and has accomplished a great deal in the direction of industrialization. An important spur to the economy has been the temporary, but large, supply contracts for United States and ROK troops fighting in Vietnam. On the other hand, President Park admits that one of the major problems still facing the ROK is the reform of agriculture. In what still remains a basically agricultural country, the farmer has gained little over the past decade.

But the most exciting development during the Park years has been the growing possibility of negotiations for a peaceful reunification of Korea. At the end of 1971 prospects looked very poor indeed. President Park had proclaimed a state of national emergency on December 6, in view of the changing international scene, including the entry of Communist China into the United Nations and the "fanatic war preparations being carried out by

Land reclamation project in the Republic of Korea.

the Communist regime in north Korea." This seemed for a time to mark an end to the talks proposed by the Red Cross organizations of both North and South Korea in August, 1971, but the Red Cross negotiations continued, culminating with the establishment of a formal agenda and an agreement to hold meetings alternately in the capitals of the two halves of the peninsula. The South Korean delegation first visited P'yŏngyang in August, 1972, and the North Korean delegation was greeted by cheering crowds in Seoul on September 13, 1972.

But in the interim, a bombshell announcement had been made. It was revealed that high-ranking officials of the North and South Korean governments had been meeting secretly and had reached a seven-point agreement as a preliminary to reunification talks.

The seven points stated in essence that national unity was to be achieved by *Korean* efforts, free of outside interference, by peaceful means, and transcending differences of ideology or systems of government; that the two sides would refrain from verbal or armed provocation; that various exchange programs would be established; that both sides would actively cooperate with the current Red Cross talks; that a direct telephone line would be established between Seoul and P'yŏngyang to prevent the outbreak of unexpected military incidents and afford a means of dealing directly with problems which might arise; that a North-South coordinating committee would be established to implement these proposals.

For the first time in nearly thirty years the wall of the DMZ had been broached by other than intelligence agents and provocateurs.

9

The Democratic People's Republic of Korea

The Democratic People's Republic of Korea came into being during the same period as the ROK. During the transition period of military government the Soviet armies in the north very realistically built on the system of committees that had been established by the Koreans to maintain civil order after the Japanese surrender. During the transition to local Korean control these "people's committees" were more and more brought under Communist control. Operating at county, city, and provincial levels, the committees in turn sent representatives who made up the Provisional North Korean People's Committee. This body unanimously elected Kim Il Sung chairman and drafted necessary legislation for the operation of government as well as adopting a draft constitution modeled on that of the Soviet Union. National elections were then held in the north; in November, 1946, a single slate of candidates to serve as delegates to a convention of the people's committees was presented to the voters. The convention, held in February, 1947, approved the legislation and constitution as presented by the Provisional People's Committee. They also elected the North Korean People's Assembly as the supreme legislative organ of the government. On the same day, February

21, the newly elected People's Assembly gave permanent status to the People's Committee and announced the formation of a twenty-man executive cabinet headed by Kim Il Sung as premier.

While there have been continuous turnovers and changes in the higher ranks of the government in the years since 1948, and a major purge in 1958, Kim Il Sung has retained his position as premier and leader of the Korean Workers' (Communist) party. The stability and continuity of the DPRK has not been threatened by internal dissent and military takeover as has that of the Republic of Korea. In December, 1972, Kim Il Sung was elected president of the DPRK under a new constitution, apparently written to provide for the new era of coexistence and reunification with the ROK. One important point in the new constitution of the DPRK is that it calls P'yŏngyang the capital of the country, thus setting aside the contention that Seoul was the only capital and P'yŏngyang was merely a temporary capital serving until reunification. That is, it recognizes that the two halves of Korea are indeed two separate nations today.

Electrified railway, Democratic People's Republic of Korea.

That is not to say there have not been problems in maintaining solidity. The Korean Communist party grew as three disparate groups: those who organized and worked in Korea itself during the Japanese occupation, those who were attached to Chinese Communist groups in Yenan in the 1930s and 1940s, and those who were centered in Manchuria and Siberia, many of them acting as guerrilla forces against the Japanese. In order to maintain his position, Kim Il Sung—who belonged to the Manchurian group and was Russian-trained—had to deal with the other two groups as well as the political organization that had been established in Korea following the liberation.

For some time the DPRK allowed two nominal opposition parties to function, but they soon became powerless. The struggle for power went on within the higher ranks of the Workers' Party itself, where Kim Il Sung had first to accommodate, then—as his power increased—get rid of the more powerful members of rival Communist groups. In 1958 members of the Korean-based Communist party were purged, that is, removed from positions of power, and the constant shifting of those in high positions soon made it apparent that the old China-based Communists were losing their influence.

In the south the army, with its highly trained administrative personnel, ultimately proved the major threat to the government in power. However, in the north, at the end of the Korean War, the military leadership was purged by the Kim Il Sung faction. This removed the blame for failure from the shoulders of Kim Il Sung. At the same time the purge served effectively to remove a potentially threatening group from positions of power.

Kim Il Sung was sixty years old in April, 1972. He has borne the burden of leadership of the DPRK since he was thirty-four. Nearly half his life has been a public one, and he has emerged a "people's hero," a "great and glorious leader," and the primary architect of one of the most resilient and self-sufficient of the small Communist states—the one about which the Western world knows the least.

Little is known of his personal life before he emerged as a leader in 1948, but the official biography suggests what went into the making of this impressive personality. Kim Il Sung was born in a village near P'yŏngyang on April 12, 1912. His great-grandfather, a small farmer, is said to have fought the opening of Korea to the West and to have been one of the group of Koreans who burned the American warship *General Sherman* when it intruded into Korean waters in 1866. His grandparents were active in the resistance to the Japanese occupation, and his father was said to have been one of the organizers of a revolutionary underground group in 1917 known as the Korean National Association.

After migrating to Manchuria, together with his family and countless other Koreans, Kim, while still in his teens, joined with the Korean guerrillas operating out of southern Manchuria. When the Japanese invaded Manchuria in 1931 he was one of the founders of the anti-Japanese guerrilla army, called by some the first "revolutionary armed force of the Korean people." The guerrilla army fought continuously against the Japanese throughout the Japanese invasion of China and the years of World War II; sometime around 1940 Kim Il Sung left Manchuria for Soviet Russia, where he received military training and rose to the provisional rank of major.

At the end of the Pacific war, Kim entered Korea with the Russian army. He was at that time leader of the Korean People's Army, successor to the guerrilla armies of before. He had strong Soviet support in his efforts to bring together the various factions of the Korean Communist movement which led to the formation of the DPRK in 1948. At that point the Soviet army announced its withdrawal and a complete return of power to the hands of the Koreans.

There is no doubt that under Kim Il Sung's leadership North Korea has made impressive gains. Even before the Korean War broke out, industrialization had begun. All industries were nationalized. Military equipment and technical supplies were largely imported from Russia, and, as in the south, huge quantities of outside aid were required.

In agriculture, major land reforms were instituted immediately. The farmers were given the rights to the land they worked (though this did not entail ownership as we know it, since these rights could not be sold, rented, or mortgaged). All large landholdings were broken up; no one was allowed to hold more than two and one-half acres of farmland. Sweeping reforms were also undertaken in education, health, and welfare services—indeed, in all aspects of society. Everything was geared to attainment of goals set by the government, and the education of the people to the government-espoused ideology and beliefs. Reforms were barely underway, however, when the Korean War wreaked almost total destruction upon industry and power supplies in the north. The city of P'yŏngyang was described as total rubble at the end of the war.

In 1954, the DPRK embarked upon a series of economic plans in an effort to restore destroyed industry. For the first ten years or so the greatest concentration was upon heavy industry: machine building, metallurgy, chemicals, and electric power. Considerable amounts of outside aid were necessary, and it came mostly from East Germany, Poland, and Czechoslovakia. By 1963 the DPRK was able to claim that it had achieved a basic industrial independence and would be able to continue industrial growth through its own technological and economic resources. By 1967 the DPRK claimed over ten times the industrial production of 1947. It was held up as a showplace for Asian communism, much as the rapid economic growth of the Republic of Korea in the late 1960s gained it the label of an Asian showplace for democracy.

Even if we qualify all these claims somewhat, there can be no doubt that the DPRK worked a remarkable recovery from the Korean War and established a firm industrial base in a very short time. Today North Korea produces tractors, buses, and electric and diesel locomotives. There are oil refineries and steel and chemical plants. Machine tool plants produce nearly all the industrial equipment required. This rapid industrialization has necessitated changes in the fundamental agricultural makeup of the country and traditional ways of farming.

At present it is estimated that around 60 percent of the population is employed in non-agricultural work. Collectivization of the farms was carried out between 1954 and 1958. There are no single family farms, but large cooperative farms that average around twelve hundred acres in size, each worked by about three hundred families. In all of North Korea there are nearly four thousand of these farms. They are irrigated, use tractors and chemical fertilizers, and nearly all are electrified. Increased efficiency in farming methods has led to both an increase in agricultural production and less need for men to work the fields. The surplus manpower has been moved to industry.

Visitors are invariably impressed with the achievements of the DPRK. There are many reasons for this, but most striking is that less than twenty years after one of the most terribly destructive wars in our time North Korea is one of the very few small nations in the world that have been industrialized. A sympathetic Western observer, the Australian Wilfred Burchett who had covered the armistice negotiations from the north and had seen the destruction in the days just after the war, summed up North Korea's progress in this way after a visit in 1968: "Chosen, 'land

Simpo Fish Cannery, Democratic People's Republic of Korea.

of morning calm,' as the Koreans call their land, is a happy country of well-fed, decently clad people in its northern half. For Asia this is almost a miracle. For an Asian country totally destroyed fourteen years ago it is an absolute miracle."

All this must be qualified somewhat. Until 1972, the DPRK was perhaps the most isolated of all nations in the world. Most reports by outside observers have been made by those basically sympathetic to the Communist regime and committed to its ends. It is only now with the general easing of tensions in East Asia, that North Korea's isolation is coming to an end. With the Red Cross meeting and the negotiations between the P'yŏngyang and Seoul governments, meaningful communication between the two halves of the peninsula has opened up for the first time since the Korean War. Only recently have American newsmen visited the north.

We should take two things into consideration in judging this achievement. First, and perhaps most important, has been the relative stability of the North Korean government as opposed to the instability in South Korea. Kim Il Sung has retained his power since 1948, and there seems never to have been any major threat to his control.

Secondly, we must realize that the central government in the north has almost unlimited power. The Korean Workers' party is the only political organization in the DPRK. This strong central control reaching into all aspects of life—from what appears in the papers or on television to what foods are available and what is to be taught in the schools—might make us feel that the restrictions on personal freedoms are too great a price to pay for the results. But again we must remember that many of the freedoms we take for granted, or feel are most important, are meaningless to a starving farmer or an unemployed worker who would have no chance to exercise them in any case.

With this said, we may characterize the North Korean political system as an orthodox Communist polity. In other words, the state (that is, the government led by Kim Il Sung and the Korean Workers' party led by Kim Il Sung) has absolute power. The Korean Workers' party stresses its allegiance to Marxism-Leninism, and uses this ideology as a means of bringing and holding together the people. Slogans like "steel-like unity" are used to suggest a unity of purpose that finds its best expression in the "thoughts of our great leader, Kim Il Sung." Many of us, no doubt, feel that we should deeply resent the kind of intellectual conformity this implies. But there is more to the system than this. On the negative side, at one extreme the individual who dissents from the approved ideology may face arrest and punishment by the police; or in self-criticism sessions among his friends and associates, become the target for disapproval and public airing of his errors or deviations. On the positive side, there are real economic and social rewards to be gained by adherence to a single doctrine. There is also the psychological or spiritual reward of feeling an important part of the process of helping the nation reach its goals. There is a strong element of nationalistic patriotism in the DPRK.

Kim Il Sung is a hero to the great majority of the people of North Korea. They are seldom out of sight of his portrait or earshot of his wisdom. He is a skillful rhetorician, often encouraging the people to identify with concrete goals by means of an appealing slogan or symbol. In 1957 a movement was launched which was given the name of a traditional symbol—Ch'ŏllima, the legendary horse that was able to leap ten thousand *li* (about three hundred miles) in one stride. Like the flying horse the North Korean people were to stride forward with unfailing steps, ignoring all obstacles along the way, to meet the demands of the state. There were times when the Ch'ŏllima worker might well have been working more for less in terms of material reward, but continued on for the ultimate satisfaction that comes with the achievement of assigned goals.

Men do not work in this way without a sense of the rightness of what they are doing, without an ideal goal that forever remains out of reach, yet ever seems presently possible. To the North Korean, that goal is national self-sufficiency—a Korean Korea free of outside interference. In 1955 Kim Il Sung elaborated his principle of *chuch'e,* which he developed further in an address to the Fourth Congress of the Korean Workers' Party in 1961. "By chuch'e we mean that in carrying out our revolution and construction we should creatively apply the general truth of Marxism-Leninism to the specific realities of our own country, and precisely and fully take into account our own historical and actual situation, our own capacity, and the traditions, requirements, and the level of consciousness of our own people."

The idea that the Marxist ideology should be in this sense subordinate to Korea's national identity is apparent in all activities, from the teaching of children in schools to performances in the national theater. There has been a revival of interest in old Korean literature, in folk songs, dances, and even traditional costume. Behind all this is a strong sense of pride in being Korean, of being something real and individual after the years of repression by the Japanese and the threat of being overwhelmed by the neighboring great powers, China and Soviet Russia.

But on a more practical level than this the chuch'e ideal has allowed the development of a system of education and control that is loosely supported by traditional family and clan practices. More than a quarter of the total population is enrolled in schools of some sort. From kindergarten up, children learn the principles of a Marxist state molded upon the principle of chuch'e, a specifically *Korean* Communist state growing out of the ideas of Kim Il Sung.

Kindergarten pupils, Nimangji Co-op Farm, Democratic People's Republic of Korea.

10

The Tradition: Letters and Arts

The history of kings and wars tells only a part of the story of any people. The greatness of a nation stands on what is left after the kings and armies are gone. "Rise and fall, all belong to destiny," says the Korean poet musing over the ruins of an old palace in the setting sun. But it is the plaintive air of the herdsboy's flute that "wrenches" his heart and moves him to words.

There is only one language spoken on the Korean peninsula today. It is believed to be derived from that spoken in ancient Silla. But neither Silla nor any of the other early kingdoms had a writing system of its own. Korea borrowed her writing system from China, along with many other things. This would not, perhaps, have led to many difficulties if Korean had been a language similar to Chinese, or if the Chinese writing system had been an alphabetic one. But in the Chinese system each symbol, or character, represents an idea, a word or part of a word, rather than a sound. For the speaker of Chinese this presents little difficulty since he has only to match the written forms with words he already knows in the spoken language. But when applied to the Korean language it was very inefficient. As a result, for the most part, while the Korean continued to speak Korean, when he wanted to record something he or someone else had said, he wrote it down in Chinese.

Some Silla scholars attempted to adapt the Chinese system to record the Korean language. But the result, called *idu,* was much too awkward for general use. Imagine trying to write an English sentence in a set of picture symbols, some of which represent meanings, some of which represent sounds only. It suggests a rebus and would present many of the same difficulties.

Chinese, called *hanmun* when written and used by Koreans, continued as the writing system for most purposes until the mid-fifteenth century when King Sejong, feeling the need for a practical way of writing Korean, appointed a group of scholars to study the problem of devising an alphabet. After years of work a totally new alphabet was developed that did not owe the shape of its letters to any existing alphabet. Today this alphabet, consisting of nineteen consonants and twenty-one vowels and diphthongs, is most commonly known as *han'gŭl.*

It is understandable that most of the literature which has come down to us from pre-fifteenth-century Korea was written in hanmun, but even after the han'gŭl alphabet had become available for use a great deal of writing was still done in hanmun.

To help understand why this was so, it might help to think of the prestige of Latin in the Middle Ages and later. It was the language that unified the intellectual world: no matter what language you ordinarily spoke, you were able to communicate in Latin with any educated man in Europe. In addition, Latin bore the weight of tradition, and the emotional weight of being the language of the accepted church.

In the same way, Chinese, especially in its formal written form, was an international language in East Asia, as well as the one in which the major works of the Confucian philosophy-religion and many Buddhist texts were written. In studying his tradition, the

Page from a manuscript book of traditional Korean poetry, written in han'gŭl with some Chinese characters.

Korean had to know Chinese. To leave his impact upon that tradition in old Korea he had to write in hanmun.

But language also had less solemn purposes. There was day-to-day life, laughter, tears, love, treachery. There was the funny story to be retold for someone else's delight, and the joy in making it even better in the telling. There were the songs and poems that grew out of simple things, from a person looking at, recording, saying something about the world and life about him, and, of course, within him. From simple beginnings in the recording of folk songs and folktales on to the writing of complex histories, novels, and poetry, Korean literature grew over the centuries. Korea's literary heritage in both hanmun and Korean is no slight one.

Though writing stories or poems was seldom the first concern of the traditional Korean author—he was a scholar first, with his duty to his state—once the government examinations had been put aside and he had retired from the world of "dusty papers," he would often turn to writing poetry, in Korean or in hanmun, for his own pleasure and that of those around him. For letters and the arts were important to him throughout the history of Korea. They were the good things of life that came to him first as a student learning, and last in the fulfillment of his age.

Before Western ideas of publication and printing were introduced, his writing usually would not be published, in our modern sense. Despite the capability of printing books in Korea, there was no great reading public, and books were not bought and sold as they are today both in Korea and in other countries. Publication of a man's works often came after his death, in many cases as an act of respect on the part of a son or a grandson who would gather together all his writings and have them printed to honor the author's memory.

The earliest Korean writings we have date from Silla. Most of them are in hanmun, but there are several poems that were written in Korean and recorded in the awkward idu system. Most of these texts were actually copied, from books which have since disappeared, during the following Koryŏ period. During Koryŏ there was a great deal of writing. There are collections of essays, anecdotes, stories, and poetry written in hanmun. There are also several long poems recorded in idu from Koryŏ's later years:

> Going, are you really going,
> Leaving me and going on your way?
> . . . . . .

I'll take hold of you—but then
If I offend you'll not come back again.

. . . .

Unhappy lord, I'll see you off,
And as you leave, so come back again.
Oh, the even tenor of our days.

An important development in the writing of fiction came from Kim Si-sŭp, 1435-1493. Unhappy with the way things were going in the Yi dynasty court, he left government service and retired to a mountain retreat where he lived out his days away from the turmoil of public life. Here he wrote the stories collected under the title *Kŭmo sinhwa*. Kim Si-sŭp did not turn to China for his themes and settings as did so many writers of his period. Rather, he wrote about Korea and Koreans. He was a social critic, disturbed at what he felt was the license of his times, and at the same time a social reformer.

Kŭmo sinhwa did not have the effect it might have had on the further development of Korean letters, however. It disappeared from Korea during the Japanese invasions of the late sixteenth century, along with thousands of other valuable books taken back to Japan by the retreating invaders. Editions of the stories were published in Japan in the seventeenth and nineteenth centuries, but it was not until the late 1920s that they were printed and made available in Korea again. This has been the fate of much of Korea's literary and artistic production in the past: when it was not destroyed by invasion and war it was carried off by the invaders, leaving behind only hints of what must have been.

After the han'gŭl writing system had become available in the fifteenth century it was easier for Koreans to write in Korean, and many authors turned to their native language. But the hold of Chinese culture was strong, and to many the Korean writing system seemed vulgar and not fitting for scholarly use. It was a response to these pressures in the society that led to the omission of many men's works in Korean when their collected hanmun works were published.

But much does remain. We have collections of short lyric poetry called *sijo* which were written in Korean during the Yi dynasty. The poems are brief, witty statements of man's position in this world, his pleasures in nature, his sorrows or loves.

> When I see her I wish I could hate her.
>> When I don't see her I wish I could forget her.
> Or, rather, I wish she had never been born,
>> Or I had never met her.
> I only hope I die before her: then she can pine for me.
>
> Poet unknown, 18th century

The Yi dynasty also produced longer narrative poems. Both these longer poems and the sijo were closely linked to music. They were more often sung to set melodies than read or recited. Literature meant to be read consisted mainly of novels and shorter narratives, many of these appearing in both hanmun and Korean versions.

There was no playwriting as we know it, for the traditional Korean theater was very different from the one we know in the West. Plays, performed both at the court and in the provinces, were a combination of music, dance, and acting. The players wore grotesque masks, and the plays were performed on outdoor stages, on the ground surrounded by the audience. The texts were an oral tradition and passed on from actor to actor, not written down for memorization. The actors were not professional in our sense any more than the Korean writers. They were mostly farmers who performed when called upon, then went back to work in their fields.

Another form of quasi-dramatic performance grew up around the eighteenth century. It was a combination of singing and recitation by one man accompanied on a small drum. Several traditional stories were told in this way, the storyteller attaining great skill in assuming the roles of different characters and in singing.

One thing nearly all these dramatic performances had in common was satire. They were popular, performed by, and most often for, the people. The scholars, the Buddhist monks, the government officials, the rich landlords, all were made fun of.

A traditional mask play.

Most of the traditional literary forms no longer exist today. A few of the plays are still performed, men still write sijo, but, with the opening of Korea to the West in 1882, a new era was ushered in. Korean writers began to look toward Western literature for their forms. Today Koreans write short stories, novels, poetry, and plays that are derived as much from our tradition as the Korean.

Koreans now write in Korean, yet even within this century it has been no easy task to do so. Korean authors were writing in Korean at the end of the nineteenth century. The power of the Chinese tradition was breaking down. Newspapers and magazines began to appear, and the audience for writers was growing. But with the coming of the Japanese, writing in Korean became a dangerous thing, because the Japanese government-general hoped to make Japanese the national language of Korea. When an author persisted in writing in Korean he was immediately suspected of holding anti-Japanese feelings. And indeed, writing in Korean was a way of affirming oneself as a Korean against the cultural aggression of the Japanese. From 1910 to 1945 Korean literature was in good part an expression of Korean national feeling against the Japanese.

The Korean language and alphabet are important to Koreans. No other country in the world has a national holiday celebrating its alphabet. On October 9 each year Korean schools and businesses close, and special ceremonies are held all across the nation to mark the development of the Korean alphabet under King Sejong in the fifteenth century. Thus, even in a time of change, modern Korea takes time to pay respects to her past.

Perhaps the best known Korean productions in the arts are the grayish-green porcelains of the Koryŏ period known as celadons. These mark the peak of the potter's art in Korea. But even before and after Koryŏ the potter's art was a great one, so great that an English art historian has called Korean ceramics "one of the summits of all ceramic achievement."

Where paintings and other objects tend to be destroyed by war, weather, and time, pottery remains. We have a record of Korean pottery from prehistoric times to the present. The prehistoric pottery was rough, but by the time of the three kingdoms much more sophisticated pots were taking shape in Koguryŏ, Paekche, and Silla.

While the potters of Koguryŏ and Paekche probably were working under Chinese influence, the Silla potters were producing a distinctive gray pottery, harder than any being made in the other kingdoms. These gray ceramics have been found mainly in tombs, as many as three hundred in one tomb. They range from simple covered cups on tall openwork feet to clay figurines. As Buddhism became more powerful in Silla, burial customs changed. Buddhist doctrine required that the dead be cremated. This practice was followed after about the seventh century, and the tombs in Silla no longer were filled with pots, so that few remain beside the burial urns in which the ashes of the dead were placed. The ceramics remaining from the later years of Silla are nearly all of this type.

In the Koryŏ period, the pottery took on simple, graceful shapes, and the Koryŏ potters developed the grayish-blue color that the Chinese of the time considered one of the world's outstanding achievements. Many of the celadons were used in temples. Others were for domestic use, in the homes of aristocrats and members of the court. They ranged from large vases with delicate designs to small cosmetics boxes. Many of the pieces had covers decorated with elaborate figures; stylized lions, tortoises, phoenixes, and ducks were common along with lotus leaves and other flower shapes.

After the Mongol invasions in the thirteenth century the great period of Koryŏ pottery came to an end. It was never to regain its creative greatness.

Yi dynasty pottery was much simpler than that of Koryŏ, yet the early Yi pots were very attractive to the Japanese, particularly for use in the Japanese tea ceremony.

The making of pottery was a village industry carried on through the centuries by families who were born to the craft. The villages were located near good sources of ceramic clays, and kilns for firing the pots stood nearby. Nearly every family would have a potter's wheel, and every village would be able to turn out on order any sort of pot, from the fine wares used in the temples and the court to the reddish pots that were used every day by the common people. The potters, despite their high artistic achievement, did not rank very high in the social scale, but if the serenity of form that appears in their finest creations can be used as a measure, their lives must have been satisfying ones, lives devoted in community to fine craftsmanship.

When the Japanese armies retreated from their invasion of Korea in 1598 they took whole villages of Korean potters with them. These potters were put under the protection of local Japanese lords. In Japan they continued to produce fine ceramics, helping to lay the foundations for the world-famous Japanese porcelain industry.

There were potters left in Korea, of course. The Yi court maintained its own kilns until late in the nineteenth century when the great tradition of Korean ceramics, as expressed by the village community of potters, came to an end.

It has only been in the years since 1945 that some younger Korean potters have again begun to work within that tradition. But there is a difference between their work and that of their artistic ancestors. These young potters consider themselves artists, creating objects for their beauty, not for use. In the past, the potter was a craftsman turning out pots for specific uses, not for decoration alone. The potter of the past was closer to those modern Korean potters who make the functional storage jars that decorate the back yards of all Korean homes with a dark brown monotony.

The tomb paintings of Koguryŏ are the oldest remains of Korea's pictorial art; they are some of the oldest paintings remaining in East Asia as well. Paekche was noted for architecture and sculpture. The few remains have been recently enriched by the discovery of King Muryong's tomb. Fine bronze statues of the Buddha and bodhisattvas, intricately wrought ornaments, and finely decorated ceramic tile remain as evidence of Paekche's achievement in the arts.

More art work remains from the Silla kingdom. Until 1971 there were no known remains of Silla painting. In September, 1971, the fourteen hundred-year-old tomb of a Silla noble was excavated. Unfortunately it had been desecrated so that no loose art objects remained, but upon the ceiling of the chamber were lotus blossom designs, much larger and rounder than those found in the Koguryŏ tombs. Though the color of the murals had faded badly, the designs of the four spirits—blue dragon, white tiger, firebird, and tortoise—were still visible in red, blue, and black.

Other Silla tombs have produced gold crowns that present an unsolved puzzle. Branching antlerlike, the gold is skillfully wrought and the crowns are hung with comma-shaped pendants of green jade and sequins. They resemble no crowns found elsewhere in the Far East. The closest things to their shape, in our experience, are the wingshaped viking helmets. Where the style originated, or how it developed in Korea, remains a mystery.

As Buddhism began to take a deeper hold on the peninsula, Buddhist sculpture and architecture became more important. Probably the most famous example of all is the stone cave known as Sŏkkuram, not too far from Silla's ancient capital of Kyŏngju. Perhaps in part modeled on the ancient stone caves of Indian Buddhism, in part on the tradition of the Koguryŏ tombs, this cave is an eloquent testimony to both the greatness of Silla's art and the profound meaning of Buddhism to the Silla culture.

Situated near the top of a ridge, the cave looks out over the Japan Sea and is so situated that the first rays of the rising sun fall upon the face of the great stone Buddha, nearly eleven feet tall, that sits in the center of the domed cave, carved out of the rock of the hillside. There is a pervading sense of peace and tranquility in the Buddha, in no way interrupted by the other sculpture decorating the rest of the cave. This was long thought to be the largest stone Buddha statue in Korea, but 1971 brought the discovery of another stone Buddha from Silla, nearly twice as large, located on a rocky cliff in South Chŏlla Province.

Silla also cast some of the largest bells the world has ever seen. These bells were not rung by a clapper, but were struck with heavy logs suspended from ropes. Thus, a bell of almost any size could still be rung fairly easily. The earliest bell that remains dates from A.D. 726 and weighs thirty-three hundred pounds. This

The stone Buddha in the Sŏkkuram.

would seem to be large enough, but a bell cast later, which also exists today, is estimated to weigh in the neighborhood of seventy-five tons.

Koryŏ's ceramics were her greatest achievement. The flourishing of Buddhism also led to the building of great temples and the further development of sculpture. One of the finest examples of Koryŏ sculpture is the Buddha of the Pusŏksa temple in North Kyŏngsang Province, central Korea.

With the decline of Buddhism and the rise of Confucianism in the Yi dynasty, the arts that had served the great Buddhist temples declined. Confucian shrines were not decorated with statues, nor were fine ceramics used in Confucian ceremonies. The major decorations of these shrines were pictures of Confucius and some of his followers. Painting became more important.

Except for the Koguryŏ tomb paintings, with their affinities to the Han dynasty art of Nangnang, we have few examples of Korean painting up to the middle of the Yi dynasty. We are told of the skill of Silla painters, and there are a few examples of the painters' art of late Koryŏ in the murals on temple walls and the illustrations to Buddhist books. But the destruction of wars and the ravages of time have taken their toll, and it was not until the early eighteenth century that many examples of Korean painting were produced that survive.

Portrait painting was considered an important art in the Confucian state and the government set up an office which maintained a number of men as official portrait painters. But their work was not limited to portraits; they also painted landscapes, pictures of animals, and men in their everyday occupations. Their models remained Chinese, but the Chinese of the Ming dynasty, and in one artist's refusal to accept the fashions of the Manchu court he seems to have also found the strength to bring out the Korean aspects of his art.

Cats and Sparrows, late Yi dynasty painting by Pyŏn Sangbyŏk.

The painter who is credited with having added this new vitality to Korean painting was Chŏng Sŏn, a man known best by his artist's name of Kyŏmjae. He is said to have painted daily for eighty years of his long life. We do not know exactly when he was born or died, but the dates commonly given are 1676-1759. Like so many of the painters of his time and later, Kyŏmjae was not a member of the aristocratic class. In his youth he showed such promise as a painter that he was helped by an aristocratic neighbor to gain a position in the office of portrait painters, and there he served for over fifty years. His painting was said to have improved as he grew older, and his contemporaries report that even when he had grown old and had to use magnifying lenses in order to work, his painting was better than before.

Kyŏmjae's major achievement was to make Korean painting Korean. He turned to the details of the Korean countryside, outlining them in recognizable form. His painting is eccentric and rough, and today critics do not find in it the greatness upon which his contemporaries heaped their praise. But if his painting was too blunt and rough in its reflection of the troubled times in which he lived, it was the trouble of Korea he was reflecting. Korean art was becoming national; the rejection of the intellectual course of the Manchu in China gave Korea a respite from the often overwhelming hand of China, and in the next two centuries Korean painting was to chart its own course.

Today painting is one of the most active arts in Korea. Some painters work in traditional styles, some attempt to mix traditional with Western styles, and some work in the Western tradition. Over the past few years several Korean painters have had one-man exhibits in such centers of Western art as Paris and New York.

Korean traditional music grew up around religion and court ceremonial. Later borrowings from central Asia and China enriched this music which underwent great development in the Koryŏ period. The Yi dynasty also offered an enlarging of the musical repertoire and a continuation of the court tradition. These traditional forms are strong and enduring. The American composer Lou Harrison wrote in his *Music Primer:* "The nobility & lyricism of Korean music is very special, very sturdy, & very close to me." It is different from the music we are accustomed to. The rhythms often seem complex and unfamiliar. Melodies are most frequently built on a pentatonic (five-tone) scale (B♭ C D F

Royal Court Orchestra preserves traditional Korean music.

G; or very roughly, on your piano, black keys only beginning with F♯). The Korean orchestra consists of unfamiliar instruments creating their own very special tone colors.

Folk songs vary in kind from work songs of the farmers and fishermen to lullabies and songs sung by girls out picking spring greens on the hillsides. Other types may have some religious significance: for example, songs sung by farmers on their way to work in the fields are meant to propitiate the spirits of the harvest.

The Koreans' natural joy in music led to a quick adoption of Western music when hymns and Western songs and melodies came to Korea with the missionaries at the end of the nineteenth century. In 1901 the court brought in a German musician to organize and train a military band. This was a great success, leading to a program of open-air concerts in downtown Seoul that continued into the early 1920s. It served as the introduction to Western music for many young Koreans.

Traditional dance grew up closely related to music, religion, and court ritual. Like the music, the dance also showed two patterns, the slow, refined ceremonial dance of the court and the free, lively folk dances. A Westerner who had the chance to see one of the court dances being rehearsed in the court in 1903 speaks of it as "radiant with color." He goes on to say that the dance was also "without motion, so slowly were the fantastic figures developed." By comparison, the folk dances were almost

Traditional drum dance.

violent. A fifteenth-century Korean described these dances: "We bob our heads, and roll our eyes, hump our backs, work our bodies, legs, arms, and fingertips." The dancers' movements were like a "twanging bow."

Associated with music and the dance are women known as *kisaeng*. Throughout Korean history, their position was different from that of other women. They were educated to be companions to men, and were skilled in poetry, song, and dance. Unlike wives, who were supposed to serve their husbands and bear their children, these entertainers could meet men as intellectual equals. With the end of the court in 1910 they began to disappear, for the old life was fading out. Today they have often become nothing more than entertainers in good restaurants.

Both the traditional music and dance are performed in Korea today. Societies and institutes have been set up to teach and preserve these arts of the past, and young students come to learn, hear, and see. But there is also great interest in Western music and dance; north or south, any metropolitan center will boast of its orchestras and provide some opportunity for the enjoyment of Western opera, ballet, and modern dance. The great artistic achievements of both traditions, East and West, stand side by side.

11

The Tradition: Systems of Belief

In every society certain values and beliefs are taken for granted. They have become a part of the fabric of everyday life and are seldom questioned. When many members of the society begin to question these values, or to act in ways opposed to them, all aspects of life begin to change more rapidly. The individual often feels lost; each man seems to be going his own way without paying proper respect to traditional ways of thinking and behaving. The beliefs and values that had once enabled the individual to maintain peace or harmony with his environment seem to disappear.

Such a change distinguishes traditional from modern Korean society. As Western ideas and beliefs have flooded into Korea since the last years of the nineteenth century, they have come to suggest different values, beliefs, and ways of acting than those commonly held before. The individual has begun to question his tradition. For, despite the wide range of class, education, and position among Koreans, traditional Korean society held more attitudes and beliefs in common than modern societies. In many cases, the differences in beliefs and values of two modern South Koreans who live and work side by side will be much greater than those that separated a poor uneducated farmer and a wealthy aristocratic landowner in traditional society. In this sense the ideological uniformity of North Korea is closer to traditional patterns.

However, although many Western ideas have been adopted in Korean life, there remains a hard core of values and beliefs that spring from another tradition, and another way of life. Basic to these values are three different sets of beliefs, or systems of thought: primitive shamanism or spirit-worship; the highly formalized ethical philosophy, Confucianism, including ancestor worship; and the theological system of Buddhism, with its hopes for salvation from the pain of existence in this world. Much later, two important religions came to the peninsula: Christianity in the seventeenth century, and a purely Korean religion, Ch'ŏn-dogyo, which grew up in the nineteenth century. But despite the importance of these religions in the lives of the individuals who follow them, they have not had as broad an effect on the structure of society as Confucianism.

The original religious system in Korea was the kind of spirit worship that we call shamanism. It is perhaps difficult for us to think of it as a formal religion, for it does not have churches, priests or ministers, or even a regular set of creeds or beliefs. All things, animate or inanimate—animals, trees, mountains, rocks—each has its own spirit. The way to the good life is to be in harmony with these spirits. There is a real sense of a spirit world with which the individual has to keep in touch. To live in harmony with this spirit world it is necessary to establish a means of communication. Some individuals, called shamans, profess a special ability to do this.

When someone is faced with a particular problem which he feels is caused by a spirit, he goes to the shaman for help. Offerings of one sort or another are made to the spirit—a chicken, some grain or cloth—and the shaman tries to establish communication by falling into a trance, often brought on after chanting and dancing to the accompaniment of a drum. Once she has established contact with the spirit an attempt is made to find out what the problem is and how it can be solved. After this has been done the shaman takes the offerings as payment.

In Korea these shamans have generally been women, although blind men also made up an important class. The importance of shamans at any period cannot be underestimated; in the 1860s a Korean queen showed great favoritism to one. Today, when all else fails, the Korean is liable to turn to the shaman. It is difficult to estimate how much belief is put in the actual performance of the shaman. There is certainly more respect for the shaman in the countryside than there is in the large cities, but even Seoul has a district where they come together, and where citizens of the city can consult them on various matters.

The most pervasive system of belief is Confucianism. But in many ways it is the most difficult to comprehend. Since its first appearance in the peninsula, which must have been at least as early as the first century B.C., the Confucian system has had an overwhelming effect. In the course of time Confucianism not only established codes of behavior for the individual, family, and ruler—linked with rituals of respect for the dead; it also provided the philosophy and system of government, and the core ideas for Korea's philosophy and a good deal of the literature. It has been said that to write the history of Confucianism in Korea would be to write the religious, social, cultural, and political history of the nation, and in a sense this is true.

There are few Koreans today who would call themselves Confucian, but the structure of their daily life, their behavior toward each other, is derived from Confucian practice. The universities may consider Aristotle more important than Confucius, but the veneration for learning that has led to the amazing development of modern education in Korea is derived from Confucianism.

Where the fundamental belief in shamanism is that the good life lies in the proper relations between spirits and humans, in Confucianism the good life is thought to lie in the proper relations and behavior between individuals. Basic to this system of values, set forth by Confucius in the sixth century B.C. in China, was a set of standards by which actions could be judged. The center was man himself. Man could become a moral "personality" or a good man through learning and self-discipline. The good, or moral, man had two main characteristics. He was humane; that is, he behaved in a proper way to the people around him. He also had a strong personal sense of moral duty. By attaining those two things a man became a good man who could make up part of a good society where his example would serve to help others achieve the same goals. Proper conduct in society was of the greatest importance.

The rules for this proper behavior were specified in a set of five relations: of son to father, of wife to husband, of younger brother to elder brother, of friend to friend, and of subject to ruler.

In practice this meant that the son must be obedient to his father, as his father must be to the king; the wife must be obedient to her husband, the younger brother to the elder, and the younger friend to the elder friend. Women are reduced to a low position, but men are expected to have a great deal of faith in each other, to be able to restrain their feelings, hold high ideals, and to approach each other with benevolence.

Among the practices of Confucianism, one that helped give it wide significance is what has been called ancestor worship. The son's duty to his parent extends beyond life. He must be obedient while his father is alive, and after his father's death he must show his respect in an extended period of mourning, and by constant

Confucian ceremony.

ritual observances on the anniversaries of his father's death.

But it is not only the father who receives this veneration. The dutiful son also pays his respects to grandfather and great-grandfather, as well as to mother, grandmother, and great-grandmother, though in a lesser degree. The ties with the past, and with the family past in particular, are given a deep emotional significance through this practice. And it becomes doubly important that the family line not be broken. The son, if he is to be a good son and good family head, must produce a son to follow him. One of the unquestioned grounds for divorce in traditional

Korea would be that the wife had not produced a son, for a son is essential to carry on the family; he is the link that ties the future with the past.

All the other relationships in the Confucian system are an extension of the father-son relationship. Loyalty to the king, respect for elders, the relegation of women to a childbearing position are all related to this desire to maintain proper relationships. Unlike other systems, Confucianism is not concerned with man's relation to eternity. There is no teaching about a god or an after life. Yet it does establish the means for a strongly ethical personal life rooted in the continuity of the family, as well as a proper political or social life rooted in the relationship of subject to king, where the king himself is thought of as a sort of father.

Buddhism, which had its origins in India, was introduced to China in the second century B.C., and from there into Korea in the fourth century A.D. In Korea it seems at first to have appealed only to scholars, but soon its interest spread to the common people. During the Koryŏ period, when Buddhist influence was at its zenith, it influenced both daily and artistic life a great deal.

Buddhism taught that life meant suffering. It said that the continuation of life, which means the continuation of suffering, is a result of our desires and our fulfillment of those desires. For the Buddhist the only salvation, and with it the end of suffering, was the total extinction of self. To attain this salvation one had to be free of desire. There was no end to life until this extinction of self was attained; all beings were continually reincarnated.

Salvation was attained in two ways. The first, called enlightenment, was through an understanding of what made up the elements of life. The other was by entering Nirvana, a state of non-being which could not be explained.

Out of these basic beliefs grew two schools of Buddhism. One flourished in Southeast Asia, the other in China, Korea and the north. Although both schools were to find their way into Korea, the northern school was the most important.

Known as Mahayana Buddhism, this school taught that salvation could be attained by the intercession of a class of beings called bodhisvattas who had reached salvation themselves, but who remained in this world in order to help those who appealed to them by faith or through acts of charity. Thus salvation could be achieved both by good works and faith.

Where shamanism and Confucianism sought to reconcile man with life in this world by setting up means to remove suffering, Buddhism showed a way to an end of suffering and life through meditation leading to enlightenment, or faith and good works. It also offered ritual in the temples, a means of release through prayer, and gave men a sense of the unimportance of the here and now.

Yet, as with all religious experience, that of the Buddhist cannot be adequately explained. On the one hand, it is one of the most highly intellectual and rational of all religions; on the other, it offers the illiterate masses relief from the pains of existence. While Buddhism seems to place little importance upon the activities of the common everyday world, its followers often find release from the petty distractions of day-to-day living and a more profound meaning and direction to their lives.

Despite the wide differences in the nature of these beliefs, they were not incompatible. A man could be Confucian or Buddhist and still turn to the shaman in time of trouble. At a time in his life when he felt the most need for getting along in this world he could turn to the teaching of Confucius to show him the way. When the pain and suffering of this world seemed overwhelming he could turn to Buddhism for a way out. It was only with the appearance of Christianity on the peninsula that the Korean was to come face to face with a religion intolerant of other faiths,

which demanded an all-or-nothing belief on the part of the pro-
fessing individual.

Christianity first received some attention by Koreans in 1784.
Christian documents were brought into the country from China
and were studied by a few scholars who then became interested
in this new learning. In time they formed a small Christian group
and requested that a missionary be sent to them.

Before the opening of Korea to the West in 1882 there was
little significant contact with Protestant Christianity. There were
only the Roman Catholic priests who had carried on their work
in the country in disguise. But even with repeated persecutions,
brought on in part by the Christian insistence that believers stop
their ancestor worship and in part by the fear of any foreign
influence, there were an estimated twenty thousand Catholic
Christians in Korea by the middle of the nineteenth century.
After 1882 Protestant missionaries began their work in Korea.

Linked with the new religion was the culture and learning of
the West, and the missionaries found that schools became one of
their most effective means of gaining contact with young Koreans.
The growth of Christianity in Korea has been linked with the
development of schools to teach Western science, languages, and
medicine, and even today two of the major universities in Seoul
maintain their ties with the missionaries. Western learning and
Christianity, or Western religion, were linked in Korean
minds.

It was in part the result of this linking that the last of the
major Korean religions grew up. The Ch'ŏndogyo, then known
as Tonghak, was founded in 1860. While the religion itself bor-
rows from all the great systems of belief that Koreans had come in
contact with up to that time, it has evolved as a distinct faith.

Ch'ŏndogyo does not concern itself with life after death.
Rather it replaces this sort of tenuous immortality with one that

can be easily understood, the immortality that comes from the achievement of the perfect personality. The person who has achieved a perfect personality lives forever, not as a spirit or through the achievement of Nirvana, but as, in the often cited example of Admiral Yi Sun-sin, the hero of the sixteenth-century war with Japan, present in the blood and memory of the Korean people.

To achieve this sort of immortality a man must live well with his fellow men, not doing anything to hurt them. By living this way he begins to achieve the perfect life. In Ch'ŏndogyo the world is divided into three levels. The highest is God, or heaven, the eternal or moving principle. The second is man himself, who is the highest of all living things and partakes of the nature of God. At the bottom of the scale are all other living things. A good man will begin to assume more and more of the attributes of God, and in the process will work toward the achievement of the perfect state in this world. The evil man begins to take on the attributes of the beasts and work toward the destruction of the perfect order.

Ch'ŏndogyo faces the world in a passive way. Change— that is, life, death, and the beginning of a new life—is the only reality. The final aim of existence is to live in harmony with this unending change. This is achieved not by action, but by inaction—by doing nothing that will disturb the harmony.

All these religions and systems of belief continue to exist in Korea side by side. Not far from Seoul the road turns into a narrow mountain valley; then, just as the valley opens into farmlands and vineyards, off to the side is a small Christian church. The building is of cheap lumber, unpainted. About a hundred yards away flows a clear stream along the foot of the mountains. Across the stream on a small level spot stands an old building in the traditional Korean style with its upturned tile eaves and pounded clay walls. This is the local shrine to Confucius. A few hundred yards down the stream, on the same side, and half-hidden in the brush, stands a small wattle hut with a straw thatched roof, the shrine of the local shaman. Nearly a mile up the mountains, along a gorge piled high with large rocks, there is a Buddhist temple perched on the side of the peak. The three oldest systems of belief are represented here today, shamanism, Confucianism, and Buddhism, together with a later import, Christianity. The only major system not represented by a building of some sort is Ch'ŏndogyo.

Well over 6 million Koreans belong to one or the other religious group, but the great majority of the population, both in the north where religion is discouraged by the Communist government, and in the south where it is openly professed, will in some ways still be Confucian. The old practices related to the Yi dynasty government have broken down, but in their daily life these people will respect the five relations, and will remain linked with both their ancestors and their heirs in the continuity known as ancestor worship. And there will always be days for many when they turn to the village shaman to bring their lives back into harmony with the spirits that inhabit objects around them.

12

The Tradition:
Fashion, Food, and Festivals

Korean dress has changed little over the centuries. The traditional clothes worn today by many Koreans are not radically different from those pictured in the Koguryŏ tombs of the fourth and fifth centuries A.D. The essential costume consists of a pair of rather loose trousers, a short coat or blouse with rather narrow sleeves, and a belt of cloth or leather. In the Koguryŏ period there was little distinction in style according to rank, wealth, or sex.

Soon, however, Korean women began wearing skirts over their trousers: over this basic costume an overcoat. Up until the end of the nineteenth century there was a great variety in the types: they could differ in color and style according to rank, wealth, and personal choice. In 1884, in order to cut down on abuse of rank, the court ordered that all must wear the same type of overcoat, a long, straight-cut coat with rather full sleeves, and this has been retained down to the present whenever traditional clothes are worn.

In this century Koreans have tended to adopt Western clothing, especially in the cities. The change has been more rapid among the men than the women, and today only rarely is the traditional Korean man's costume seen on downtown city streets, even though it is common in the countryside. Women have not changed their dress so rapidly. True, the streets of Seoul are filled with women dressed in the latest fashions from New York or Paris, but side by side with them will be many in their flowing skirts and short blouses.

The traditional Korean color for clothes has been white, and the material most commonly used is cotton. However, the modern Korean lady has a great variety of materials and colors from which to choose. These are still, however, limited by season, her age, and how much she can afford to spend on clothes. A young woman might well dress in a scarlet silk skirt and glossy black blouse in the winter, but as she grows older she will change to more subdued colors.

High school students, Republic of Korea.

There is less variation in the farm woman's dress. She wears full length skirts topped by very short blouses, both most often of white cotton. Her shoes are straw sandals or of rubber. Her hair is long and tied in a knot at the back of her head, and she wears little or no makeup.

In the cities men tend to be seen in their traditional clothes more in the winter than any other time of year. The winter clothes are quilted and much warmer than Western clothes. But even in the summer the Korean man who rushes through the city streets in a Western business suit will often change into the loose-fitting Korean costume when he gets home at night. Again there is some variety in color, though white still predominates. There will be no bright colors, but conservative shades of blue and gray do appear. Over the trousers, blouse, and vest the long flowing overcoat is most often black, though occasionally a gray-blue. The modern addition to the traditional costume is inevitable. This three-pocketed vest has been copied after the Western vest and is worn over the blouse. It will sometimes add the touch of color to an otherwise very conservative costume.

In P'yŏngyang and the cities of the north there is much less variety in dress. Most of the men wear dark trousers with white shirts (usually tailless) while the women are dressed in dark skirts with white blouses. Most of the children are in neat school or organization uniforms. Plastic shoes seem to be the rule, although sandals do appear. A great part of the clothing worn in the north is made of vinylon, a synthetic fabric developed by a Korean.

The farmer is typically dressed in white. His trousers have full legs and a crotch that falls near the knees and gives them an appearance of almost falling off; they are tied around the waist with a cloth belt. He also wears a white, long, and loose-sleeved blouse over which he may have a vest. He probably does not wear

Farmer Plowing. Late Yi dynasty painting by Kim Hong-do.

socks, but he may have on a pair of rubber shoes, shaped something like toy boats, or a pair of sandals woven from rice straw. This is his traditional dress, but in these times of change his everyday wear might be different. He might be wearing an old army uniform or work clothes. The farmer's hair is cut short, much shorter than a crew cut, all over his head, and his scalp is as tanned by the sun and wind as are his face and hands.

A lot of bright colors are limited almost exclusively to children's clothes. Today, in city and country both, children's everyday wear tends to be more and more like our own except that during the school year they wear their school uniforms. But on holidays they will be dressed in traditional clothes, cut exactly like those of their parents. The great difference is in color, as the blouses will be striped in green, yellow, and red and the trousers and skirts will be equally colorful, though usually of one color.

Korean food is distinctive. Every meal is served with rice, the staple. The foods that are taken with rice vary greatly according to area, family, and economic group. Rice is frequently mixed with other foods in Korea. Often it is mixed with barley or millet, or with beans, and especially on special occasions, with chestnuts. Other grains, especially barley and millet, are boiled and served like rice when it is not available.

Meals are usually served on small individual tables, with a rice bowl, a soup bowl, and other dishes for sauces and side dishes. Chopsticks and a spoon are used for eating. The chopsticks are not as long as those you might find in a Chinese restaurant, nor as short as those in a Japanese restaurant. Chopsticks are used to pick up most solid foods, although the spoon may be used for rice. The spoon itself has a round, very shallow scoop with a narrow handle, often oval in shape. Most commonly, both chopsticks and spoon, as well as many of the serving dishes, are made of brass.

The basic Korean meal consists of rice and the pickled cabbage called *kimchi*. Next to rice, kimchi is the most important item on the Korean menu. It adds spice to the meal in summer and is one of the few vegetables available in winter. Every housewife has her own special way of preparing kimchi and the taste will vary greatly from house to house. Until you have learned to savor kimchi in all its various forms you will not have really learned to appreciate Korean food.

There are three basic kinds of kimchi: that made with cabbage; that made with the large white radishes we find in our stores under their Japanese name, *daikon*; and that made with cucumbers. The basic ingredients are the main vegetable, salt water, hot red peppers, green onions, garlic, leeks, and mashed-up small shrimp or fish. The kimchi may be dressed up in many ways. Family taste and finances determine what other ingredients might be added. Octopus, squid, meat, piñon nuts, chestnuts, pears, apples—alone or in combination—each adds its own distinctive flavor.

When the cabbage crop is in, in the late fall after the first frosts, all the efforts of the women of every household, city or country, are turned to making the winter's supply of kimchi. An average family of seven or eight will probably purchase from 80 to 100 heads of cabbage plus a straw bag, about a bushel, of daikon. This should make enough kimchi to last from late November until the end of February or early March. In the city this is also a time when money is apt to be a little short, for all available cash has to go into the purchase of winter supplies. Some employers even give what is known as a "kimchi bonus" at this time of year, a little surplus pay to help meet the extra expense.

Once the cabbage and radish have been purchased or harvested, the real work begins. The cabbages are stripped of dead leaves and washed on the *madang*, the court or front yard of the Korean house, then put in tubs of brine to soak overnight; this is to take the freshness out, or "kill" the cabbage, as the housewife would say. While the cabbage is soaking, the other ingredients will be prepared. The next day—or days, depending on the amount of kimchi to be prepared—is spent stuffing the cabbages and coating the cubed daikon with this mixture. After the cabbage is stuffed it is placed in a large earthenware crock. When the crock is full the contents are weighted down with a heavy stone.

The crocks are either buried in the ground or set inside a cool storage room to keep them from freezing or getting too warm. Either can spoil the kimchi.

Cucumber kimchi has a place all its own. Unlike our pickles it does not keep, but from the time the first cucumbers appear in the late spring until they are all gone in the fall, cucumber kimchi adds taste and variety to the menu. The stuffing is nearly the same as for the other kimchi. Small cucumbers are slit on three or four sides deeply enough that the slashes meet. The stuffing is put in the slits, and the cucumbers stand to age for two or three days. Then they come to the table and the supply is soon gone.

Cucumbers are also preserved for winter use. This is done by placing them in a jar with a good deal of coarse salt, weighting them down, and letting them stand. Though not as tasty as the cucumber kimchi, they too are a welcome addition to a winter menu that has almost no fresh vegetables to offer.

Soups play an important role in the Korean meal. There is great variety in soups. Many are made with no meat at all. A simple soup might be made of soy sauce, bean sprouts, and water, perhaps with some bean curd cakes added. More elaborate soups might have beef or chicken, perhaps some potatoes. Another group of soups, which we might call stews, have a lot of red pepper. To a base of a red pepper paste and water are added bean curd, fish, kimchi, or other available meats and vegetables to give the soup substance.

Two special soups should be mentioned. A soup made of dried seaweed, and usually some meat, is always eaten by a woman after she has given birth to a child. It is also served at birthday celebrations. The other soup is linked to the New Year and is always eaten on New Year's Day. This is a rich beef broth with oval slices of a special rice cake made from steamed ground

Home economics class, Republic of Korea. Long bamboo chopsticks are used in food preparation.

glutinous rice. Often, the soup also contains small dumplings stuffed with meat, bean curd, bean sprouts, and kimchi.

Meat is scarce and expensive in Korea. Beef, pork, and chicken are all eaten, but not as everyday foods. However, one beef dish is nearly always on the table when a Korean family entertains a foreigner and is one of the fond memories that many Americans have of Korean food. This is the broiled beef called *pulk'ogi*. Thin sirloin slices are marinated in a mixture of soy sauce, sesame, sugar, onion, and garlic. Then they are broiled over a charcoal fire on a special domed rack. The perforations on this rack are punched out in small inverted crescents so that all the juices lost in cooking run down into a trough around the edge, which is usually partially filled with water, to make a delicious gravy that can be spooned out as the meat cooks.

The seas around Korea supply a great variety of seafoods which make up an important part of the Korean diet. Oysters, shrimp, clams, and abalone are available; octopus, squid, sea cucumbers, and seaweeds also are eaten, as well as many kinds of fish, both fresh and salt water.

Deer, wild boar, ducks, and pheasants are common in Korea, and although they do not play an important role in the diet, they are eaten.

An important food that may substitute for rice and essential on most holiday tables is noodles made of wheat or buckwheat flour. We have our noodles, macaroni, and spaghetti from Europe, thanks to Marco Polo who learned the art in the Chinese court of the great Khans. Noodles in Korea came from the same source. They may be eaten hot or cold. A marvelous lunch on a hot summer day in Seoul is cold buckwheat noodles, heaped high in a bowl with sliced pork, plenty of red pepper, and kimchi and ice, a dish available at special restaurants. But it really is a winter dish. In the past, winter was the only time of the year when there was ice.

Korea also produces a wide range of fruits and vegetables that are eaten in season. Few foods are preserved by canning or freezing. Lettuce comes in the spring along with other vegetables, such as spinach, chrysanthemum shoots, and wild greens. Strawberries are early, too, followed by a variety of melons, plums, pears, apples, mandarin oranges, grapes, delicious persimmons—very different from the sour variety we know—jujubes, and chestnuts.

In Korea, as everywhere, good food and holidays go together. The holiday year is really divided in two; holidays that are associated with the traditional Chinese lunar calendar, and those that follow the official calendar which is the same as ours. The lunar calendar is made up of twelve months based on the phases of the moon. To keep the months and seasons in proper relation an extra month has to be added every few years. By this calendar the new year begins in spring, with the New Year falling in late

January or early February. For example, in 1965 the first day of the first month by the lunar calendar fell on February second by our calendar.

The New Year is the most important holiday by the lunar calendar. Festivities last for fifteen or sixteen days, from the first of the month until the first new moon of the year. On New Year's Day everyone gets up early. Traditionally, one must first pay respects to the spirits of the ancestors. Then a round of visits begins, paying respects to relatives and neighbors. To the children especially this is a good time, because for each New Year's bow they may expect in return a coin or a gift of candy or food. Their elders are more apt to be offered a cup of rice wine.

The fifteen days are a period of relaxation for the villager, but in the city life and work go on pretty much as usual. During this time men and boys fly kites; women and girls, both in village and city, play a special kind of jumping game on seesaws. The seesaw is placed on a block about a foot high. One girl stands on one end, and the other jumps on the other end, shooting the first girl up into the air. They continue, leaping higher and higher, their full skirts flowing around them as they go up and come down.

A day known as Hansik comes during the second month. Only cold foods are eaten on this day. Many families visit the tombs of their ancestors and make offerings of cold noodles, wine, and other foods, which they eat after a ceremony at the tomb.

The eighth day of the fourth month is the Buddha's birthday. Dressed in all their holiday best, the Buddhist members of the community form lantern-lighted processions, wending their way to the services at the Buddhist temples. As the long processions wind along to a major temple, the candles flickering through the paper lanterns make a most impressive spectacle.

Although it is not celebrated much in the city today, the fifth day of the fifth month remains an important holiday in the

Ceremony marking the Buddha's birthday.

countryside. It is called Tano, and in the past was linked to the expelling of bad spirits and the cleansing and purifying of the family for the summer that lies ahead. The combination of two fives also was believed to be lucky. On this day there are contests for the girls in which they match their skills in swings suspended from the trees, and wrestling matches and other contests for the young men.

The fifteenth day of the eighth month is also a major holiday. It is a sort of thanksgiving for the good harvest; a time to pay respects to the ancestral tombs, cut the grass there, and see that the tombs are in good repair; a time for games and for relaxation from the heavy labors leading up to the harvest.

In the eleventh month, on the day of the winter solstice, usually the twenty-first of December by our calendar, it is customary to eat a special porridge made of red beans. In very traditional homes the porridge is also sprinkled on the grounds to help ward off evil spirits.

The major Korean holidays by our calendar are of a different nature. They do not originate in the cycle of the farmer's life, the Confucian practice of ancestor worship, or folk belief. Rather they tend to celebrate national events as many of our holidays do.

The first of March is celebrated as Independence Day in memory of the March First Independence Movement against the Japanese in 1919. August 15, Liberation Day, celebrates Korea's release from Japanese control on August 15, 1945, with the end of the Pacific war. There are many more days, both north and south, which take on special importance with respect to some particular event in the past.

People celebrate other occasions that are not linked to the cycle of the year. These are the festivities that surround the major events in life, birth, marriage, and death. But changes are taking place in these observances, and what might be true of the village will not be true of the city; what is true of the south may not be true of the north.

There is very little celebration at the time of birth, though the new father's pride, especially if it is a boy, is bound to show through. The new baby and mother are kept in isolation from all but members of the immediate family for three weeks. Then relatives and close friends are invited in to have a look at the new child. When they come they bring small presents, and are usually offered some food and rice wine before they leave. One hundred days after the baby is born the same visit is repeated. The party this time may be fancier, but the preparations depend very much on the situation of the family.

The first birthday is a most elaborate celebration. The baby is dressed in full traditional costume and formally introduced to the guests rather than simply viewed by them as before. It is at this point that the child enters into society.

A special table is prepared for the occasion on which various items linked with different occupations are spread. There are a writing brush for the scholar, some coins for the businessman, needle and thread for the housewife, and so on. The child is placed before the table and the items he chooses are supposed to indicate his fate in life. A meal of rice, special seaweed soup, and other delicacies is served. As the guests leave they will be presented with some dainties wrapped in paper, and they in turn leave some money in a plain envelope.

Birthdays continue to be celebrated throughout the life of an individual, but none of them assume anything like the importance of the first birthday until he reaches the venerable age of sixty. In traditional Korea a person who has lived out sixty years has lived his full allotted span; from that day on he becomes a kind of living immortal.

The sixtieth birthday celebration is usually a large one, generally larger than the family can afford, for how well it is carried off is an indication of the respect the children have for their parent. The person being honored will be seated in front of the room behind a table piled high with dried persimmons, rice cakes, and other fruits and dainties. Then, one by one, the immediate descendants, starting with the eldest son, will come forward and present their bows. This is a full bow, with knees on the floor; the hands are extended in front, palms forward with the fingers just touching, and then the head and hands are brought down until the hands touch the floor and the forehead touches the hands. After the bowing a glass of rice wine is presented to the person who is sixty. This continues through all members of the family in the order of closeness of relation, on down to close friends and well-wishers. After the formal ceremony has come to a close the party is liable to extend well on into the night.

Marriage customs today vary widely, some areas in the country keeping the traditional ceremony nearly intact, others keeping it in part; in the cities, wholly new patterns of weddings have grown up.

The traditional marriage procedure was unvarying. The bride and bridegroom had nothing to say in the selection of their mates. All arrangements were in the hands of the parents and the go-between who took care of the details. A wedding was an elaborate and expensive affair involving ceremonial visits between the families and a trip by the groom to his bride's home to bring her back to his parents' house for the culmination of the wedding ceremony. In the past the full ceremony belonged to the upper classes. Today, even among their descendants, it seldom takes on its full form. In the cities the modern wedding hall has simplified the elaborate preparations formerly made in the home for secular weddings, and many marriages take place in Buddhist temples or Christian churches. The wedding hall ceremonies are roughly patterned after Western church weddings; there are generally a best man and bridesmaids, dark suits and formal wedding gowns. Though a clergyman may officiate, more often the wedding is carried on by some respected friend of the groom's father. A good part of the ceremony is taken up with the long address he gives, exhorting the newlyweds to proper behavior. For the reception after the wedding the bride frequently changes to her traditional Korean dress.

When it is known that a parent is going to die, all the children try to be present. It is a mark of disrespect to one's parents not to be with them as death approaches. In the more traditional families, once death has come the women will begin a long wail. One of the close male relatives will then climb on the roof, usually carrying a shirt belonging to the person who has just died, and shout out his name three times. This is to call the soul of the dead person out of the house. There will be no sleep the first night after the death, and in most families there will be no sleep for immediate members of the family until after the burial. The first night the women let down their hair and wail loudly. The men join in, though not so violently.

Burial always comes on an odd-numbered day after death, counting the day of death as one. It usually takes place on the third, fifth, or seventh day, although it may be delayed longer in special cases. Preparations for the funeral start soon after the death. The women begin to sew the mourning clothes, a coffin has to be obtained, and refreshments have to be prepared for the friends and relatives who come with condolences for the family.

Two days after death the body is dressed in good clothes, or special burial clothes. The body is placed on a plank that has been set up at the place of honor in the room with a folding screen placed in front. As soon as the coffin is ready the body will be transferred to it.

When preparations for mourning are completed a mourning feast is prepared, the family as a unit bowing before the coffin. On the chosen odd-numbered day, the body is taken to the cemetery and buried.

Funeral processions with colorful hearses are seldom seen in the cities now, though they are often seen moving away from a village toward a hillside cemetery. The traditional hearse is made of a wooden platform placed over two carrying poles. It is covered with a canopy, and painted in several different colors. Blue and red cloth add color to the decoration. After the coffin is prepared to go to the grave another offering of food is made to the dead. Then twelve men, six on each side, pick up the hearse on which the coffin has been placed and make their way toward the cemetery. A funeral song is sung as the hearse moves along, while the relatives who accompany it keep up a steady wailing.

After the coffin has been lowered into the grave, and the grave has been filled level with earth, another food offering is made, and the family as a unit again bows to the dead. When the relatives return home they place a paper with the name and date of death of the person together with a photograph, if available, with the ancestor tablets, then make another food offering, another bow, and the funeral is over.

The period of mourning is not over, however, and on the date of death for the next two years a food offering and ceremonial bow will take place. After that, respects will be paid to the deceased along with the other ancestors on the New Year and the fifteenth day of the eighth month.

13

The Village

Korea is a land of farming villages. Unlike the United States, where farmhouses sit far from one another in the middle of the farms, the farmers live in houses set close together, usually on the southern slope of a high hill or mountain, and go out to their fields to work each day. Many of the villages are set far off main roads, and farm families often have to travel several miles to market their goods and buy many of the things they need.

The staple food of Koreans is rice, and most villages face out onto lowlands covered with rice paddies, cut off into a jigsaw design by the dikes that hold the water on the fields and separate them. Water, and lots of it, is essential for growing rice, and the paddies can only exist where there is a good water supply from streams or irrigation projects. The higher fields, where water is not as available, are used for other grains, principally barley, and vegetables. These are known as dry fields.

There is little grazing land and only a few animals. Several houses will have an ox; there are some chickens perhaps, and a pig or two, or even a few goats staked out on the dikes or back on the hillside. There may be some dogs; these are not pets, but are used for hunting or as watchdogs, or they are being raised to be eaten during the hot days of summer when dog stew is supposed

Village in the Republic of Korea.

to have a tonic effect against the exhaustion brought on by the sun. Cats are rare, almost never seen in the villages.

The hills, or mountains, to the north of the village supply it with fuel in the winter, not often from the trees themselves, but the underbrush, branches, and the pine needles that are raked and bundled for fuel. Wild greens and vegetables are gathered here also. The cemetery is usually on the mountain, higher up than the village; some families have private cemeteries.

Agriculture in Korea, and rice culture, in particular, is intensive, aimed at gaining the highest yield from the available land. Machinery has seldom been used for tilling, planting, or harvesting, and even in more recent years it has not been used to any great extent in the south though tractors and machines are widely used in the north.

In order to get things done on time in the rapid course of the year it is necessary to pool labor. The farmers in the villages work together in transplanting the rice, in weeding and harvesting the fields. It is important for them to live close together to be able to help each other. Villagers must also share their labor for essential projects such as digging wells, maintaining irrigation ditches and reservoirs, or even building and maintaining local roads.

Although the water supply is not usually a problem, for the hills behind the village act as a reservoir of ground water, wells have to be dug. Usually a group of houses shares one well—although a rich farmer may have a well within his garden—as well as the labor of digging it, keeping it clean, and any other maintenance that it might require.

The well is an important spot in the Korean village. There the women gather in the morning to draw their water for the day, and their graceful carriage as they carry the heavy water jars on their heads back to their houses is one of the unforgettable sights of the Korean countryside. The well is also a social center for housewives. There they do their washing, squatting on the ground and pounding the wet clothes with flat sticks as they exchange news and gossip. In the daily life of the village there is little time left after work for social gatherings for the young woman.

The houses of the village will usually be clustered together, opening out onto a path, or a road if the village is lucky enough to have one. The smaller village, and over half the villages in South Korea are made up of fewer than one hundred families, may simply be lined up along the path, while the larger village may spread out with side paths running off the main path or road.

Three things that can be seen immediately tell a great deal

about the economic well-being and social position of the families in these South Korean villages. Tile-roofed houses with stone walls are those of the wealthiest. Next come the larger thatched houses with stone walls, and then the thatched houses with wattle fences.

Despite differences in outside appearance all the houses are built on the same general plan. A typical house is L-shaped with four rooms for living and one, or perhaps more, for storage, or, if the family owns an ox, a stall. In most villages the front of the house is open, but in the rear there is a fenced-in, closed-off area that can only be entered through the kitchen—a sort of garden that belongs mostly to the women of the household.

The room at the short bottom of the L is the kitchen. It has a dirt floor that has been dug out several feet lower than the rest of the house. Along the wall that lies against the rest of the house— that is, the wall that is at the inside corner of the L—is the stove. The stove is made of stone and clay and looks like a shelf running the full length of the wall. It is about a foot-and-a-half high, two-and-a-half feet wide. Set into it are two or three large iron pots, the largest around two-and-a-half feet in diameter. These are the cooking vessels. The large one is used to cook rice, and the others are for the preparation of other dishes. Today these pots are sometimes made of aluminum. Under the pots is an opening for feeding fuel to the fire, controlling the draft, and raking out the ashes.

The stove is placed in this seemingly awkward position because of the heating system of the Korean house. The kitchen stove is used to heat the adjoining room at the bottom of the long side of the L. Flues from the kitchen fire run under the floor of that room to a chimney in back, heating the floor on the way. A room heated in this way is called an *ondŭl'pang*.

The corner room that these flues heat is a sort of master

bedroom, as well as the private family living room. Guests are seldom invited into this room. The floor, in order to receive the heat from the flues, is of a special construction. A series of dividers made of clay and stone are covered with large flat stones. These in turn are covered with clay in order to get a smooth flat surface, although today cement is becoming more common as it distributes the heat more evenly. Over the clay or cement is a layer of heavy yellow-brown oiled paper that has a warm finish like well-polished hardwood when it is in good condition. This floor serves as bed and chairs for the family.

The room seems bare by our standards. On the side facing the kitchen is a wall cabinet which projects out over the kitchen stove and reaches up to the ceiling. It is used for storage. At the other end of the room is a wooden cabinet, on top of which the quilts that are used for the bed will be rolled during the day. There will probably be one window, high on the side wall, perhaps with glass panes, but more probably covered with translucent paper. The walls may be papered, but just as often they will be bare smoothed clay.

The next room, in the middle of the long side of the L, is a wooden-floor room, as distinguished from the paper-floor room just described. This room is not heated, as it does not have any flues running under the floor. For most of the year it serves as a dining room–living room for the family. It is here that guests are received. Nearly all of the front wall forms a door; in the back wall, looking out on the enclosed garden, there may be a small window or a wooden door which can be opened but is seldom large enough to walk through. The wooden floor generally extends a couple of feet out under the eaves, making a sort of porch where people can sit to take their shoes off or put them on, for shoes are never worn in a Korean house. Again furnishings are at a minimum: a few mats to sit on, an ashtray or two, a clock, perhaps some pictures or wall hangings, or another small cabinet.

At the very top of the long side of the L is another paper-floor room which serves as the men's quarters and as another bedroom. Since most families consist of at least six or seven persons these two bedrooms would seem a minimum, but there are many houses which have only one. This bedroom is heated in the same way as the other, with flues under the floor, but it has its own separate firebox in the front and a chimney in back.

There are several common variations of this house. If more bedrooms are needed they may be added on to the top of the L. Or another L might be built facing the first one so that there is an enclosed court between the two. In that case the second L

Courtyard in a village house. The wooden-floor room is in the center.

serves for extra bedrooms and storage rooms, but does not dupli-
cate the kitchen. In northern Korea the houses are often rec-
tangular, consisting only of the bottom of the L without any
partition between the kitchen and bedroom, for every bit of heat
needs to be conserved during cold winters. In the past North
Korean houses were often of log construction with shingled or
thatched roof, in contrast to those of clay and wattle construction
typical of South Korea. Another common pattern is a U-shaped
house which adds two or three rooms out from the top of the L,
leaving an open court enclosed on three sides. Often one of these
extra rooms is a dirt-floor room used as a stall.

There are two areas outside the house proper that are of major
importance to the Korean family. One is the private garden that
extends from the kitchen. This is not a garden in our sense,
although there might be a few gourd or squash vines growing up
the wall or fence in the summer, and perhaps a few potted plants
and some flowers. But most important to the life of the house is a
row of large glazed brown earthenware jars. The largest of these
will be around four feet tall, the smaller ones only five or six
inches. They are used for the making of the soy sauce and other
sauces that are so important in Korean cooking, and for storing
the kimchi which is the winter staple of all Korean families.

In front of the village house is an area of hard-beaten clay,
often nearly as large as the house itself, called the *madang*.
Nothing grows here, but for half the year this is the center of the
villagers' lives. It is here that the grain is threshed and winnowed
after the harvest, here that the vegetables are cut and dried or
prepared for storage. And here the family is found on a sultry
summer evening, stretched out on straw mats, or on the ground,
to get what cool air they can, often accompanied by small smok-
ing fires of green grass or weeds to keep off the mosquitoes. This
is where the men work and where they get together and talk.

Here the children play, and here the old people sit during the long days doing what tasks they can.

Somewhere near the house will be a small square outbuilding, generally covered with thatch, standing over an open pit. This is the toilet. Inside is no bench and mail-order catalog as you might expect from its American counterpart. Rather you find that, quite simply, one of the boards has been left out of the floor. Nor is there any bathtub or sink. Bathing is generally done either in the small enclosed garden or, in the warmer months, in a nearby stream.

Most of the families living in any one village will be likely to have the same name. When this is the case it is called a clan village. However, clan is a deceptive word. It means that all these people claim a common ancestor sometime in the remote past, often the person who first settled where the village grew up.

The clan relationship is important in two ways. It serves as a way of holding people together, and it determines the pattern of marriage. No members of the same clan can marry. This means that in a clan village the men will bring their wives home from somewhere outside the village, and the daughters will leave the village when they are married.

Often the clan will own lands, the profits from which are used to pay for funerals or festivals connected with ancestor worship, or to help a needy member over hard times. This has been the traditional core of the village, but in these days following the disruptions of wars and the mass movements of people there are few villages that are "pure" clan villages. The essential unit is now the family.

When we think of a family we normally only consider the mother, father, and children. This is not true of the Korean family. Many of the houses in the village have three generations represented, sometimes even four. When the eldest son of a family marries, he brings his wife home with him to live in his family home. So long as his parents are alive they will live there also. His children in turn will stay there, and should his eldest son marry before the grandparents die, his wife and family also will be under the same roof.

Because of this pattern it is easy to see why in any village the majority of the men and very few of the women have been born there. The daughters have been married into families of other clans, probably in other villages; younger sons usually have had to go off to the cities in search of a living; only the very well-off families have enough land to set up both the eldest son and his younger brothers in housekeeping. But even though the younger brothers and the daughters leave the home there are generally five to ten people living in each family house.

Relationships follow the Confucian pattern. In practice this leads to the father being isolated from his children and even from his wife. He is the head of the family, the disciplinarian, and the one to whom all loyalty is due. Making all major decisions, he carries on the family business with outside society, and does so often without much consultation with wife or children. A fully traditional father would not think of consulting them, although he might turn to his father or some older man in the clan for advice.

Although today women have the right to vote and, particularly in the cities, are going into the professions, under the traditional pattern they had no real equality with men. They were, and are, to be loyal to their husbands first of all, but loyalty was not enough. They must also bear children, and in traditional Korean society a woman is hardly thought to have borne a child until she has borne a son. The son is necessary to carry on the family, to maintain that continuity of past and future that is so important in the Confucian system.

The importance of childbearing is perhaps shown best in the way a young married couple are addressed by those around them. Before a child is born the man is called by his given name, and, in effect, treated almost as a child still. As soon as a child is born the parents are known as his mother or father and are never addressed in any other way. They have now become full-fledged members of the adult community.

But despite the seemingly unequal position of the woman, she does have considerable power within the home, if not outside. It is she to whom the children turn with their troubles, she who determines the food and clothing and the operation of the household, and often in the process she will keep tight hold on the family purse strings. Even though she is restricted by her position from associating with any men outside her family, she does associate with the other women of the village. It is up to her to keep the vegetable garden and the dry fields in order while her husband is concerned with the rice crop. And even there she works beside her husband in the rice paddies. She may not have her hand in all aspects of her husband's life, but she helps shape and sustain it to a very large extent.

As a woman grows older she is liable to take a more active part in the social life of the village. She may begin to smoke, to intrude herself on the men's councils, and attempt to get her hand into more of the operation of affairs than has been open to her in the past. This is in keeping with the Korean respect for age.

The daily life of the villagers revolves around their fields. In South Korea the agricultural year is based on the Chinese lunar calendar. The first half of the first month is the New Year's holiday; then the year's work begins in earnest. For the next month men will be fertilizing the dry fields with night soil, raking leaves and pine needles on the hills for fuel. Before the end of the second month barley, red peppers, and pumpkins are planted. In the third month the rice fields are fertilized with compost, plowed, and the seed beds for the rice planted. By the middle of the next, the fourth month, the rice is ready to be transplanted into the paddies. In the fifth month comes the barley harvest. At the same time the rice paddies have to be cultivated. In the sixth month, grass is cut on the dikes between the paddies and in the hills to be mixed with ox and pig manure for the next spring's composting of the rice paddies. The seventh and eighth months are taken up with the weeding of the rice paddies and the harvesting of various vegetables. In the ninth month comes the rice harvest and the virtual end of the agricultural year. For the next three months the farmer will be busy with

A farmers' band traditionally performs when rice is transplanted.

other things: weaving straw mats and sandals, repairing his house, and doing other chores.

In some ways winter is the easiest time for the villager. The rice crop is in. The fresh vegetables are stored and preserved or sent to market. For the time being there is no pressing concern with food and no pressing work in the fields. As the winter draws to a close, however, the rice may begin to run low. The first spring months are often marked by a shortage of food that is only relieved when the barley comes ripe in the fifth month. Rice is the great staple food of Korea, but barley fills empty stomachs when the rice supply is short.

A North Korean poet has eulogized Kim Il Sung as having made it "June in January" in the countryside. That is to say that the traditional idle days of winter are no longer wasted; changes

The rice harvest.

in agricultural methods, electrification of homes, and mechaniza-
tion have made it possible to work the year around.

The village in the DPRK today shows a marked contrast to
traditional patterns. The same is true to a lesser extent in the
south where there is an increasing use of machines and modern
agricultural techniques. However, while the government of the
ROK admits that there must be an agricultural revolution to
keep food production in line with the increasing population and
growing industrialization, and to improve the life of the farmers,
the government of the DPRK claims already to have effected that
revolution.

With the collectivization of farms in the mid-1950s the whole
pattern of village life in North Korea changed. Observers de-
scribe these villages, rebuilt or newly built after the Korean War,
as attractive, with tile-roofed brick houses surrounded by fruit
trees. One cooperative farm not far from P'yŏngyang consists of
630 households (that is, families) living in individual apartments, totaling eleven hundred persons. Each of the newer apartments for a four-member family has four moderate-sized rooms
(as opposed to two in the older ones), a toilet, and a small
kitchen. There is a central heating system that runs under the
floors. Electricity is available and every house boasts a radio and
television set.

This is a rather large cooperative, 3,000 acres as against a
national average of around 1,200. To work this land the farm has
102 tractors, 7 trucks, and 1,000 trailers. It is geared mainly to
grain production, rice and corn, but also produces vegetables,
fruits, and hogs. Fertilizer is available and used; irrigation has
removed the ever present threat of drought.

Among the services supplied in the village are a nine-year
school, a technical school, four clinics, and eighteen doctors. In
early 1972 a new hospital was under construction.

Tractors at work
in North Korean fields.

    While this is no doubt a showplace cooperative, it still serves to show the radical changes that have taken place in the traditional village structure in the north. Building on the tradition of cooperative labor, mechanization and technical innovation have completely changed the traditional life style.

14

The City

Life in the city does not follow the regular pattern that governs the farmer's life. The cycle of the seasons is broken, and summer or winter, the day goes on much the same. The patterns of life are determined by occupation, vacations, and the pressures of making a living.

Traditionally the two great cities of Korea were Seoul and P'yŏngyang, and they remain the most important metropolitan areas, although with increasing population and industrialization in both the north and the south other large metropolitan areas have grown up. Both of these cities were severely damaged by the Korean War. Both have rebuilt, but on radically different patterns.

Seoul, which has been the capital of Korea since 1392, and has remained the capital of the ROK, is a sprawling megalopolis where the skyline changes rapidly with what has been called the "frantic pace of building." A metropolis of more than 5 million today, it is a city of both the old and the new. Much of the downtown is characterized by atomic-age international style in architecture and planning. But every so often the old creeps through and gives it that touch of individuality and depth of character that makes for fascination in both cities and persons.

There are old palaces, ancient royal tombs, fortresses, the gates of the old city wall, and much else that remains and reminds of ancient Korea.

There is also all the rush and bustle of the modern city, and all the fumes and fears of environmental pollution that come with a technology that seemingly cannot plan except for its own destruction. People go in all directions of a morning: businessmen off to their offices; clerks, secretaries, shop girls all rushing to make their bus or trolley connections; schoolboys and girls in uniforms off to class. Taxis dash in and out of traffic honking their way through the crowds and cars. There is seemingly no reason or meaning to all this movement of man and machine.

At the turn of the century, Seoul was a city of around a quarter million, and even then it was growing out of its environs. The population had spilled over the wall that Yi Sŏng-gye had built around his capital city five centuries before. Today most of that wall has disappeared except for sections running across the mountains to the north and south of the center of the city. The two great gates that still remain, Namdaemun, the great south gate, and Tongdaemun, the great east gate, today stand in the center of the city.

Seoul is a city of palaces and universities. Yet here too tradition strives against the changes that are being made. The Sunggyungwan University stands beside the palace grounds where kings lived and ruled, where prince and princess played in the gardens, and the royal family enjoyed the changes of flowers through the year and the fall colors of the autumn. In Yi times the Sunggyungwan was the highest center for study in the nation. It was there that the principal shrine to Confucius was maintained. To the Sunggyungwan also came the best of the young scholars from the local schools to complete their studies under the tutelage of the greatest minds of their times.

Downtown Seoul today; view across the Duksoo palace grounds.

Today the Sunggyungwan is a modern university, offering
courses much the same as you would find in any college of arts
and sciences in the United States. True, it has a college of Oriental
philosophy where there is a strong emphasis on the study of
Confucianism, but the only real reminder of its illustrious past is
the national shrine to Confucius on the university grounds where
the elaborate ceremony honoring him is held each autumn.

Most of the Republic of Korea's major universities and colleges
are in and around Seoul. As government service in the palaces
spurred young students on to study in the past, so the chance of
getting into one of the major universities in Seoul spurs on the
young student today.

Seoul is the cultural and political center of the Republic of
Korea just as P'yŏngyang is in the north. Here are the major
offices of government, the headquarters of the armed forces, the
center of the movie industry, the homes of artists, musicians, and
dancers.

Theaters show both Korean and imported films. The Drama Center with its well-designed modern stage and facilities offers productions of Shakespeare, Eugene O'Neill, and traditional and modern Korean plays. The Municipal Theater has concerts by symphony orchestras, while the National Music Institute has concerts of traditional court music.

Department stores and special shops meet many of the needs of the people. But the great shopping centers are the two large markets around Namdaemun and Tongdaemun where everything from old books to fresh squid is out for sale in open-air stalls. They are filled with the cries of the vendors calling their wares and the excited haggling of housewives trying to bring down the prices of the fresh vegetables. The crowds surge back and forth from early morning until late at night.

The blocks in Seoul are long and irregular, particularly in the residential areas, and houses seem to be crowded together in terrible confusion. The gates leading into many houses open out only on a narrow path, wide enough for a peddler's handcart, but often too narrow for a jeep. These streets branch off in all directions, sometimes dead-ending in the middle of a block, or circling back on themselves and coming out close to where they began. Unless you know your way, or have plenty of time for exploring, it is wise to ask for directions once you leave the central areas of the city.

The houses in Seoul outside the central business area, are mostly in Korean style, much like the simple village houses. They are surrounded by walls, usually of pounded earth or of boards, and in some newer homes, of cement. Most of them are tile-roofed.

There are other styles of houses in the city. During the Japanese occupation whole areas where the Japanese lived where built up into two-storied Japanese houses with floors of straw matting.

Most of these houses were destroyed during the war years. There is also a sprinkling of houses patterned after Western-style architecture, with wooden floors, stoves, tables, and chairs.

But even as the styles of housing change, and many of the newer houses, while they are built in Korean style, utilize a space-saving square shape, the hot-floor heating system remains. No matter how untraditional the house, there will always be a hot-floor bedroom. On a cold winter's day no bed can compare to quilts that are warm through from the floor beneath.

P'yŏngyang today is described as a city of broad avenues and well-tended streets. The greater part of the city proper has been rebuilt over the past twenty years, but construction has been more controlled and directed than that in Seoul. There is none of the frenetic rush toward construction; observers seem most impressed with the calm and deliberate planning involved.

While the early morning streets in this capital of the DPRK are busy, they present a somewhat different sight from those of Seoul. There are buses, trucks and bicycles, but hardly any automobiles except for a few Russian-built cars reserved for special government use. Workers, often shirtless, jog or walk in formation along the broad streets on their way to work, singing or chanting. The children march briskly in loose formation on their way to school, singing patriotic songs. The buildings that in South Korea or in the West would house businesses, here are apartments for the workers.

There appear to be adequate goods in the shops of P'yŏngyang, but none of the variety, nor any of the luxury items that can be found in Seoul. Most shops accommodate late-shift workers by staying open until ten in the evening.

There are posters everywhere. Indeed it is said that nowhere in the north can one be long out of sight of a representation of Kim Il Sung. The posters are mostly calls for loyalty, denunciations of

Ch'ŏllima Street, P'yŏngyang, the capital of the Democratic People's Republic of Korea.

United States imperialism, and slogans of the revolution. There is no advertising such as clutters the thoroughfares of cities in the south and so much more of the world, for this is not a competitive economy; the government determines what is to be produced, in what quantity, and how and where it is to be sold.

Near the National Theater there is a park where children play as they wait to enter to see a performance, or to rehearse one of their own. There is much emphasis on pageantry and group activity here. People are brought together to see performances of traditional Korean dance and music, but also to see and participate in the drama depicting the successes of the revolution and the victory of Communist right over imperialist wrong.

P'yŏngyang is an older city than Seoul. Its past greatness dates from before the five hundred years of the Yi dynasty when the capital moved south. While the North Korean capital does preserve and revere the remains of its past, its eyes are more on the present and future.

The contrasts between the two capitals are often extreme. Seoul gives the impression of an unpruned plant sprawling every which way, including up; P'yŏngyang, a sense of ordered and planned development. Where the hurrying crowds in the streets of Seoul suggest confusion and aimlessness, those of P'yŏngyang reflect an ordered purposefulness that we often hear described as regimented. The cities themselves reflect two very different styles of life that have developed out of the political and philosophical differences between the governments of the Republic of Korea and the Democratic People's Republic of Korea.

15

Here and Now

Village or city, north or south, after the war came to an end in 1953 the major task of all Koreans was to pull together what was left. Fighting from 1950 to 1953 brought wholesale destruction to Korea: factories, railways, ports, cities, and farming villages lay in the path of the contesting armies as they surged north and south the whole length of the Korean peninsula. In the years of uneasy peace that followed, Korea had to rebuild at a terrible cost.

Today there are few visible reminders of the war. Here and there a gutted building still stands. Other buildings are pocked with the scars of rifle fire, but even cities like Seoul that were in good part reduced to a shambles during the war now assume the face of modern cities. New buildings, freshly paved streets, modern factories have sprung up over the piles of brick and rubble of only a few years past.

But even though Korea built again out of the ashes of civil war and political division, the stark reality of the demilitarized zone (DMZ) separating North and South Korea remains ever present in Korean minds. Roads leading into the demilitarized zone suddenly stop, their end marked by chains and warning signs. The railroad that once linked Pusan and Seoul with the Trans-Siberian Railway and the capitals of Europe is cut by the demilitarized zone; a derailed locomotive lies rusting, a symbol both of the violence that created the demilitarized zone and the corrosive distrust that has maintained it.

For despite Koreas' long history, the reality of the here and now is division. Each Korean must live with this burden, the knowledge that his country is divided, that families and friends, neighbors and lovers have all been set asunder by the politics that govern men and the struggling ideologies that confuse the world. Hearts must break in that harsh world governed by the politician and the general.

Unification must come. Every Korean feels it. But the Korean has not been the master of the destiny of his peninsula. The large outside powers have often intervened, and amidst the presence of foreign troops and the dominating claims of foreign powers, Korea may well have felt again like a "shrimp caught between two fighting whales."

Today there is hope that Koreans are going to take their destiny into their own hands. The leaders both north and south have long urged the reality of a Korea for the Koreans although the means favored have been different. By the 1970s the world situation has changed. The United States and the Soviet Union are not the implacable enemies they once were; American relations with mainland China have relaxed, and old tensions are loosening. Both North and South Korea, so long protected and pulled by the great powers hovering around them, now find themselves essentially alone. And finding themselves alone they have begun to come to their own solution for their own problems.

The North and South Korean Red Cross are meeting on a regular schedule in Seoul and P'yŏngyang, attempting to work out the problems of communication between members of families separated by the DMZ after the war, and the possibilities of communication and travel between the two halves of the peninsula. At the same time high-ranking officials of both governments have met and begun to negotiate means for the ultimate unification of the nation.

No one can believe that solutions will be found overnight. There are too many differences. Two generations of school children have been educated to believe that everything the other half of the peninsula stands for is wrong. There is bound to be suspicion and distrust. There will be those who will resist reunification for fear of losing the power and influence they now hold in their own half of the nation. But there seems little doubt that the first steps have been taken. The sense of the Korean people that they belong to the same nation, share the same history and culture, and will have the same future, is on its way toward realization around the conference table.

Hope renewed: the delegate of the Korean National Red Cross, Yi Ch'ang-yŏl (right), greets his North Korean counterpart, Sŏ Sang-ch'ŏl (left), across the conference table at Panmunjŏm.

Index

Some of the different romanizations (spellings) which you are likely to come across in other books about Korea have been included in the index of this book as cross-references.

158INDEX

Racial origins, 16
Railroads, 55, 56, 154
Rainfall, 12-13
Red Cross, 78, 85, 155
Religion, *see* names of religions
Republic of Korea (ROK), 68-78
  agriculture, 76-77, 145
  Chang government, 72-73
  city life, 147-151
  education, 148-149
  Park government, 75-77
  reunification question, 77-78, 85, 155-156
  Rhee government, 68-72
  Supreme Council for National Reconstruction, 73-75
  villages, 145
Reunification question, 77-78, 85, 155-156
Rhee, Syngman, 56, 64, 68-72, 75
Russia, 10, 49
  aid to Korea, 54-55
  Korean War, 62-64
  war with Japan (1904), 56-57

Sculpture, 26-27, 99-101
Seasons, 13-14, 142-144
Sejong, King, 42, 90, 96
Seonggyungwan, *see* Sunggyungwan
Seoul, 14, 60, 64, 73, 78, 118, 147-151, 153-154
Shamanism, 108-109, 110, 113, 116
Shang dynasty, 19
Sijo, 94, 96
Silhagpa, *see* Sirhakp'a
Silla, kingdom of, 22, 27-32, 90, 92, 97, 99-100, 101
Sinla, *see* Silla
Sirhakp'a, 46, 49
Sŏhak (Western Learning), *see* Catholicism

State examination system, 35-36, 43
Student riots (1960), 70-72
Sui dynasty, 28
Sung dynasty, 34
Sunggyungwan University, 148
Supreme Council for National Reconstruction, 73-75

Taewŏngun, the, 48-50, 53
T'ang dynasty, 28-29
Tangun, 18-19
Timber, 15
Tombs, 24, 97, 99
Tonghak (Eastern Learning), *see* Ch'ŏndogyo
Truman, Harry S., 64

United Nations Command, 64-65
United Nations Temporary Commission for Korea, 63-64
United States of America, 49, 55, 62-64, 72

Villages, 133-146

Wang Kŏn, 32, 34
Wilson, Woodrow, 61
Wiman, 20-21
Women, 106, 110-112, 141-142
Writing system, 42, 89-93

Yi dynasty, 41-58, 94, 98, 101, 103, 116
Yi Ha-ŭng (Ha-eung), *see* Taewŏngun
Yi Seong-gye, *see* Yi Sŏng-gye
Yi Sŏng-gye, 39-41, 58, 148
Yi Sŭng-man (Seung-man), *see* Rhee, Syngman
Yi Sun-sin, 43-44, 115
Yi Tae-jo, *see* Yi Sŏng-gye
Yoenam, *see* Pak Ch'i-wŏn
Yun Posun, 72, 73, 75

About the Author

S. E. Solberg's interest in Korea began in 1953, when he spent sixteen months there with the U.S. Army. After his return to the United States he studied Korean language and culture and received his M.A. degree in Far Eastern languages and literature at the University of Washington. In 1960 he returned to Korea with his wife and daughter and continued graduate work at Yonsei University in Seoul. While the Solbergs were in Korea they lived as a part of the Korean community and had little contact with other Westerners. Two of the five Solberg children were born in Korea.

Mr. Solberg returned to the University of Washington, where he completed his Ph.D. in comparative literature with a dissertation dealing wtih the Korean poet Han Yong-un. His translations of poems, essays, short stories, songs, and plays have appeared in *Korea Through Her Arts, East-West Review, Comment* (Manila), *Literature East & West,* special Korean issue, and other anthologies and journals. Under the sponsorship of the Asia Society, he has edited an anthology of Korean literature, which will be published by the University of Washington Press. At present Mr. Solberg is on the staff of the Institute for Comparative and Foreign Area Studies of the University of Washington. He is working on a book of the collected poems of Carlos Bulosan, the Philippine-American writer.